"A Neat Desk Is A Sign Of A Sick Mind"

Mab Graff Hoover

ACCENT BOOKS

Denver, Colorado

ACCENT BOOKS
A division of Accent-B/P Publications, Inc.
12100 W. Sixth Avenue
P.O. Box 15337
Denver, Colorado 80215

Copyright © 1981 Accent-B/P Publications, Inc.
Printed in the United States of America

Library of Congress Catalog Card Number: 80-65057

ISBN 0-89636-047-4

*The incidents are real;
the names have been
changed.*

CONTENTS

Phonophobia

"How was your first day at work?" my husband asked.

"Hard!" I moaned, kicking off high heels. "My shoulders feel like they're on fire!"

"You're not used to typing all day. Sit down and I'll rub your back." His strong fingers dug into the sore spots on my shoulders and neck.

"But you know," I went on, "I think I'm really going to like working in Personnel. Isn't it amazing how the Lord worked it out?"

I was referring to my new friend, Alice. Recently she had started coming to our church. I had invited her to join the choir and she had accepted. We sat together in the alto section, and when I shared with her our need for extra income she encouraged me to brush up on shorthand and typing and apply where she worked, The John R. Jenkins Engineering Company.

The day I applied Alice and I had lunch in the cafeteria.

7

"How did you do on your shorthand test?" she asked. Her brown eyes seemed to have flecks of gold in them and her curly red hair was always neat. She looked the part of an executive secretary.

"Not too bad considering how scared I was."

"I remember how scared I was too," she laughed. "Who will you be working for?"

"A Mr. Larson, the recruiter for designers and engineers."

"Sure, I know Howard. He's nice."

"He seems nice. But one thing he said worries me. He said his last secretary quit because she couldn't take the pressure."

My husband patted my shoulder to indicate the massage was over.

"Was there as much pressure as your boss said there would be?"

"It was a madhouse!" I turned to look at him. "I think part of the problem is because the offices are so crowded. It's such a gigantic building you'd think there would be enough room for everybody in town. Alice has a big office, but where I work all the secretaries are jammed by twos down the center of this one room. The recruiters work in little cubbyholes at the sides."

"Who is the girl you sit by?"

"My space-mate is Sharon Green. She's a doll— about twenty-one. Sort of 'Dutchy' looking—like a Vandyke painting. Big blue eyes, perfect figure, and a high, babyish voice. But—" I rolled my eyes significantly, "she's no baby!"

"Maybe the Lord has put you beside her for a reason."

8

"I'm sure the Lord is the farthest thing from her mind. But she was a good teacher today and helped me do everything with no problem—well, just a little problem."

"What problem?" my husband asked, warily.

"The phone. I've never had to use one with a lot of buttons and I got a little mixed up." I bit my lip. "I interrupted a couple of Mr. Larson's conversations—"

"Oh, oh!"

"And I disconnected a couple of people when I tried to transfer—"

"Are you kidding?"

"And I lost one person when I put him on hold—"

"You'll get fired the first week!"

"And I accepted a long-distance, collect call." I smiled. "But other than that, I had a fantastic day!"

Sometimes I wonder if I am a little uncoordinated. I also wonder if being a wife, mother, Sunday School teacher and domestic animal trainer is enough background for this job.

Dear Lord, I'm a little bit scared. I need You. Have You put me beside Sharon for a purpose? Then help me with the phone so I won't seem stupid.

"As I was with Moses, so I will be with you; I will never leave you or forsake you. Be strong and courageous . . ." (Joshua 1:5b, 6a).

"I can do everything through him who gives me

strength" (Philippians 4:13).

". . . we have the mind of Christ" (I Corinthians 2:16b).

What Goes Up

"The elevator I was on got stuck!" Sharon squealed as she slammed down an expense report on her desk. Her face was white and her eyes were bigger and rounder than ever.

"You mean just now?" I asked.

"Yes! I've never been so scared in my life! Seven minutes we were hanging up there." She plopped into her chair and pushed her hair back. "Next time I'm taking the stairs to Accounting, even if it is on ten!"

"So far I haven't had to go up there."

"You will." She took a deep, shuddering breath. "All of us are supposed to hand-carry these reports."

I began to worry. In the first place I am afraid of heights, and in the second place I get claustrophobia. And as a Christian I am ashamed of my fears.

"Maybe it won't get stuck again," I suggested. "After all, this is a new building. Everything should be in A-1 condition."

"All I know is that from now on I'm taking the stairs."

Me too, I decided. But that same afternoon Mr. Larson told me to rush up to Accounting with some figures they were waiting on.

10

It took all the willpower I could summon to make myself get into the elevator. Five people got on with me at ground level. No one said a word and the atmosphere was tense. By the time we got to the fourth floor everyone had escaped but me.

With ghostly quiet the doors closed and I began to rise, faster and faster. The walls seemed to press in on me and I felt smothered. The cell lurched and swayed. Suddenly it stopped. Oh! It had happened. I was trapped. Would they ever find me? The elevator gave a shudder and sank an inch or two. The cable had broken! Was I ready to meet my Maker? I lurched toward the control panel and was about to poke the "emergency" button when the door slid open and a young man stepped in.

Oh, thank You, Lord! You've sent someone to save me!

Before I could sob out my thanks he pushed the "9" button, the door closed and we moved up again. It took me a stunned ten seconds to realize the elevator hadn't stalled.

Just as I had figured in the first place, in a new building everything would have to be in A-1 condition. Even the stairs from ten on down were in perfect order.

Why am I afraid? Isn't my faith real?

Dear Lord Jesus, I'm so ashamed when I'm afraid. It's as though I am telling You that You aren't strong enough to take care of me. Forgive me, Lord.

11

Increase my trust.

"Have no fear of sudden disaster . . ." (Proverbs 3:25).

"When I am afraid, I will trust in you" (Psalm 56:3).

Lead Us Not

Today I've been at the John R. Jenkins Company an exciting week! I love Personnel. Everyone is friendly and a little zany. It already seems like family.

One of my favorite people is the College Representative, Roberta (Bobbie) Simmons. She is the funniest, most audacious person I've ever known. She's pretty, too—five feet four, almost skinny (oh how I wish I was that skinny), enormous grey eyes, and although her square teeth protrude slightly, she has a full and pretty mouth. She is almost always laughing, usually at someone. She is divorced and a dedicated women's libber. She's constantly reminding us that we are *women*, not to be put down.

"This is what I mean!" she yelled one day when she was studying a chart. "This word *manpower* should be changed to *personpower*! Idiots! And *draftsman* should be either *drafter* or *draftsperson*!"

She can't tolerate being called "girl" and makes fun of the housewife role. When she meets people she extends her hand like a man and punctuates everything she says with swear words.

"Shame on you, Bobbie," I said one day after a shocking stream of words had gushed out of her mouth. She strolled over and looked down at me. For just a moment I felt afraid. After all, she is one of the bosses. But I stared back.

"If you don't quit swearing," I insisted, "the Lord will have to punish you."

She hesitated and there was a tiny light in her eyes. Then she turned, and as she walked away she called over her shoulder, "Oh, *She* wouldn't do that to me!"

We're completely opposite, Bobbie and I. Yet I feel drawn to her. I'm going to have to watch it, though, because she is so funny and cute that I find myself not only laughing at her naughtiness but adding to it.

Lord Jesus, help me be a good testimony. Help me to love Bobbie as You do, but not to take part in her humor.

"Do not let any unwholesome talk come out of your mouths, but only what is helpful for building others up according to their needs, that it may benefit those who listen" (Ephesians 4:29).

Plan Ahead

Now that I'm working one thing I'm going to have to do is plan ahead. Somehow I've got to make myself decide what I'm going to wear each day, then check it out.

Yesterday morning was terrible. I had planned to wear a frilly pink blouse I had borrowed from Mother, so I put it on, fixed my hair, then put on the only black skirt I own. I looked very nice, except that when I turned to the side I saw the pink blouse peeking through a rip in the seam of the skirt.

As I yanked it off I mumbled, "Maybe I can wear black slacks."

After I had zipped them up I didn't like the way the blouse looked either tucked in or hanging out. With trembling fingers I unbuttoned the blouse and tossed it on the bed alongside the skirt. Time was whizzing by. I reached for an old favorite, my multi-striped sweater.

I yanked it on, combed my hair again, then looked at myself. The stripes were red, green, white and brown. I groaned. I couldn't wear brown with black! I pulled off the slacks and threw them on the bed which now looked like a dry cleaners shop on Monday morning.

I pulled on red slacks. Too tight. Green slacks. There was a coffee stain on the right leg. I rushed to the bathroom and scrubbed at the spot. Minutes flicked by but the stain wouldn't budge.

Back in the bedroom I threaded a needle, grabbed the black skirt and sewed up the rip.

Later in the day I called Mother. "I've got lots of

compliments on your pink blouse."

"I'm glad," she said. "If I have anything else you want to borrow, you're welcome. I know it takes a lot of clothes when you have a job."

It's going to take more than clothes. I'm going to have to make myself plan ahead so I know exactly what I am going to wear. I'm going to check each garment for spots and rips. Then I won't have any more terrible mornings.

But what shall I wear this morning?

Dear Lord, it's not just my wardrobe that gets disorderly, but my mind also. Please help me to be more organized on the outside and filled with Your intelligence and peace on the inside.

"For God is not a God of disorder but of peace. . . . everything should be done in a fitting and orderly way" (I Corinthians 14:33,40).

Gainfully Employed

I had hoped when I went to work I would lose weight. I thought I would be too busy to even think about food, and there wouldn't be the temptation of snacks in the refrigerator. However, there are snack machines everywhere in this big building. Besides that, we have a list of all the department's employees and their birthdates, and it's the custom to bring goodies for each person's birthday.

At least once a week since I've been here our department looks like refreshment time at a High School Sing. And unfortunately we are also allowed to eat at our desks. As a consequence, I've not only gained a pound this month but I may be in trouble.

Yesterday I was eating a big, chewy, caramel-coconut square when the telephone rang. I tried to swallow but couldn't. The phone kept ringing and I kept chewing. Sharon glanced over at me with a question mark on her face. On the fourth ring I picked up the phone and tried to speak. "Pushunaow!"

There was silence. Then guardedly, "Who is this?"

I kept chewing as fast as I could with my teeth stuck together.

"Misher Larshung'sh shecushari," I mumbled.

There was another long silence. Finally, in a neat, British accent I heard, "Kindly tell Mr. Larson that Mr. Perryman would like to see him as soon as possible."

I nodded rapidly.

"Are you there?" he called.

"Yeshuh!"

Mr. Perryman, the Vice President, probably thought he was talking to a moron. He came down to Personnel shortly after that, stared at me, then went into Mr. Larson's office and closed the door.

So far I haven't been reprimanded for answering the phone while my mouth was full, but I wouldn't be surprised. I haven't eaten anything at my desk this

16

morning—except one very small cookie.

Even babies don't have to eat all the time. What's the matter with me?

Dear Father, I'm disgusted with how much I eat and drink between meals. I can't really imagine the Lord Jesus snacking all day. Help my body be more like His glorious body.

"But our citizenship is in heaven. And we eagerly await a Savior from there, the Lord Jesus Christ, who, by the power that enables him to bring everything under his control, will transform our lowly bodies so that they will be like his glorious body" (Philippians 3:20,21).

The Hammer

I am amazed to find out so many in Personnel are interested in the Bible. So far I've learned that Marlene, Bea, Terry and Mr. Fitzgerald are "religious." I discovered this because I decided to bring a Bible to work—partly as a testimony, but mainly to keep me in line. I put my old King James up on the shelf over my desk along with Company Policy, Secretary's Handbook and Webster's Dictionary.

Mitzi, the receptionist, was the first to notice it.

"Hey!" she shouted. "A Bible! How *neat!*"

Mitzi is four feet eleven and wears size five, but her voice belongs to an Amazon.

"You're a Christian, right?" she boomed out above the clatter of half a dozen typewriters.

"Yes," I murmured. "You too?"

"You better believe it! Have you met Jim Jorgensen?" She looked at the ceiling and smiled. "He's a really *neat* Christian! I'll introduce you."

She spun around and clapped her hands. "A Bible at work! How *neat!*"

My face felt hot as I glanced at Sharon. She stared at us, her blue eyes inscrutable. Was there contempt in her glance? I felt a little ashamed, then ashamed of being ashamed. Neither one of us said anything until lunchtime.

At noon Mitzi appeared with a huge fellow beside her. He looked about thirty-five, with light brown hair, bushy sideburns and a crooked smile.

"Jim, this is the gal I was telling you about," Mitzi said with a pixie grin. "See? There's her Bible."

Jim's big face crinkled and his green eyes were almost lost in his tremendous smile.

"Praise God," he said softly. "Fantastic!"

He stopped by my desk almost every day after that, even though he was a busy executive in Wage and Salary. I soon learned he loved Jesus, loved the Bible and loved his fellow employees.

Yesterday when he stopped by I said, "Jim, why don't you teach a Bible class at noon?"

He looked as though I had kicked him in the shins. When he could get his breath he said, "I've been arguing with the Lord about that for weeks! I don't

18

feel qualified."

"Moses didn't think he was qualified either," I reminded him.

"Yes, but God sent Aaron to speak for him."

Just then "Bodacious Bobbie" sauntered up to him. She moved her shoulder around in a phony, seductive way and whispered, "Are you still praying for me, Big Jim?"

"You know I am." He had a tender look on his face.

"Might as well forget it. My ex-mother-in-law said I was doomed for hell!"

She pranced away on her spike heels.

Jim looked at me and the sadness in his eyes must have matched the Lord's when He said, ". . . How often I have longed to gather your children together, as a hen gathers her chicks under her wings, but you were not willing."

Jim let out his breath in a loud sigh.

"If you want to pass the word around to those who might be interested, let's meet in my office next Tuesday at noon." He smacked his fist into his hand. "I think we better get that Bible class started."

Oh, Bobbie and Sharon! Now what will you think of me?

Dear Lord, now that I've openly shown I'm Yours, help me to come "all out" for You. Please use me in spite of my sin, my willfulness.

" 'Is not my word like fire,' declares the Lord, 'and like a hammer that breaks a rock in pieces?' " (Jeremiah 23:29).

Tempered Temper

My boss makes me so mad! Evidently he has had some bad experiences with secretaries because he doesn't trust me. No matter what I do he keeps checking up on me to see if it's being done, or if I'm doing it properly. I've made a few mistakes since I've been here but I've also had quite a lot of business experience and it's belittling to have him hover over me and question every little thing.

His constant nit-picking makes me feel inept and then I do make mistakes. For example, this morning he called me into his office to show me I had put the wrong code on a form we have to type up for every new employee.

"This man is a Principal Designer and you've coded him as a Senior Draftsman." He looked as worried as a bloodhound. "That's a serious mistake."

"Oh, for goodness sake! I'm so sorry," I wailed. "I don't know how I did that. I know better." I felt terrible as I picked up the sheet to make the correction. Just as I got to his door he stopped me.

"You see, if you let that go through they might not catch it in Records and then he wouldn't get the right salary."

"I know. I'm so sorry."

"You see, it would feed wrong information into the computer . . ."

"I know that." I turned to go.

"We have to learn to continually check our work," he went on, and I knew he wouldn't quit until he had his oration out. I leaned against the door facing and unconsciously began to run my fingers up and down between the door and the frame.

I had said I was sorry. I *was* sorry. Why did he have to go on and on? Suddenly I realized my hand was caught. I had worn a large dinner ring to work and I was trapped like a monkey with his hand in a coconut.

Mr. Larson droned on, "So we must ever strive not to make mistakes."

How had I made this mistake, I wondered, as I pulled, twisted and pushed my fingers in an effort to get loose. I knew I shouldn't have worn that dumb ring to the office!

"Dear Lord," I prayed silently as I struggled to look intelligent, "You got Daniel out of the lion's den. Please get my hand loose."

Even before I was through praying my hand slipped out and I tottered backward a step. Mr. Larson didn't seem to notice, but got up and followed me to my desk. He reached for Company Policy and turned to the section on codes.

"See?" he said as though I were a child. "Here are the codes."

Only because I caught a glimpse of the Bible was I able to keep silent. But there were ugly thoughts in my mind.

I guess I'll have to wait until Mr. Larson goes to lunch to get my ring from behind his door.

Lord, I'm sorry I got so angry. I'm sorry I wore that big ring. And I am really sorry I made that mistake. I've been a poor testimony.

"Your beauty should not come from outward adorn-
ment . . . Instead, it should be that of your inner self,
the unfading beauty of a gentle and quiet spirit . . ."
(I Peter 3:3,4).

Stars and Gripes

"You were pretty ticked at Mr. Larson, weren't
you?" Sharon observed at lunch.

"He gets to me sometimes," I admitted. "What do
you do when you get mad at Mr. Dudley?"

"I never get mad at him," she said. "I think the
reason we get along so well is because we're both
Taurus."

"You're what?"

"Taurus. We were born under the same astrological sign. When were you born?"

"December fifth, but—"

"Okay, that's Sagittarius, and when was Mr. Larson—"

"But, Sharon, I don't believe in astrology."

"You don't believe in astrology?" an astonished
voice behind me asked. I turned to look at Mr.
Dudley. "Why," he went on, "I wouldn't do any
business without first reading my horoscope for the
day."

"See?" Sharon smiled up at him. "That's why we
get along so well. We have the same traits. We're
both neat—"

"Aggressive, well-organized," he added.

"Yes, but the fact you both have these qualities couldn't be because of the stars," I argued. "It has to be the way you were raised—" I looked at my desk, thought of my fanatically neat mother and added, "or something."

"Oh, no," Sharon insisted. "It's the stars. I've proved it." Her blue eyes were unrelenting. "You could at least try it."

She handed me a newspaper column. "Read under Sagittarius."

I read aloud: " '*You can be in control. State your views firmly.*' Hmm, maybe I'll tell Mr. Larson how I feel. '*But maintain your cool and curb your tendency to talk too much.*' Oh, oh! I'd better wait. '*However, don't give in to your natural bent to procrastinate.*' All right! I'll tell him how I feel this afternoon. '*Avoid arguments at any cost—remember, silence is golden.*' Oh, for—"

I gave the paper back to Sharon. "This is just a bunch of contradictions. The Bible says—"

"The Bible! Talk about contradictions!" Sharon smiled at me. "I gotta run to the bank. See you later."

Dear Lord, I'm such a poor witness! I don't believe in astrology yet I couldn't seem to tell Sharon why. Help me find the answers and give me the opportunity to show her The Way.

"Always be prepared to give an answer to everyone

who asks you to give the reason for the hope that you have" (I Peter 3:15b).

Car Pool

At choir practice a couple of weeks ago Alice and I decided to car pool. I enjoy riding with her and it has cut our gasoline bills in half, but I can't seem to get to our meeting place on time. I get up early enough but something unexpected seems to happen every day.

Yesterday for instance I had already backed down the driveway when I remembered the brownies I had baked for Sharon's birthday. After I turned off the engine, ran back into the house and got the brownies, the dumb car wouldn't start again.

It finally did get going, but by then I was ten minutes late. When I opened Alice's car door she wouldn't even look at me. We rolled along in silence for a couple of minutes, then I apologized.

"I don't blame you for being mad, but I *had* to bring goodies for Sharon's birthday."

After I explained everything she relaxed a little but she was still pretty hostile.

"You're just not organized," she scolded. "You should have everything you plan to take—your lunch, purse, whatever—by the front door."

I nodded mournfully and made a vow to myself I would never be late again.

"This freeway is too congested to drive at this

hour," she went on, "so next time you're late I'll go on without you."

This morning I had everything organized and I was even about five minutes ahead of schedule. When I opened the front door to leave, Cocoa, the idiot dog I was taking care of for a girlfriend, streaked across the threshold and disappeared into the early morning fog.

All the way to our meeting place I practiced different ways of saying it:

"Say! You'll never guess what happened . . ."

"I'm sorry to be late, Alice, but Cocoa ran out the door . . ."

"Have you ever taken care of a dog for a friend . . ."

Alice was right about the freeway being too congested to drive when you hit it a few minutes late. I plan to go up to her office on morning break and I hope when I explain about the dog and how lonely it was in the car she'll agree to continue our car pool.

Dear Jesus, why is it so hard for me to be on time? If I was going to share the ride with You, would I be late?

"The King will reply, 'I tell you the truth, whatever you did for one of the least of these brothers of mine, you did for me' " (Matthew 25:40).

"In everything, do to others what you would have them do to you, for this sums up the Law and the Prophets" (Matthew 7:12).

Saturday, The Deceiver

"Come in!" I yelled over the clunk, clunk of the washing machine.

"You're at it early," my neighbor said as she eased a pile of dirty clothes to one side with her foot.

"Saturday is the only day I have, now that I am a *career person.*"

"I know," she said. "That's why I'm here. I'll go to the store for you if it will help."

"Oh, bless you. But I have too much to buy." I opened a closet and took out oil paints and easel. "But I'll ride with you to save gas."

"You're going to paint today?" she asked as she looked at the stack of dishes, the messy living room and the clothes to be washed on the floor.

"Sure. Everyone needs a hobby. Can you wait a minute while I take the sheets off the beds? Come with me."

In the bedroom I opened the sewing machine.

"You're not going to sew!"

"A little." I showed her a pattern and material. "I want to get started on this. I need clothes."

"But you can't do so much in one day!"

I smiled confidently. "The day is young and I'm a fast worker."

By the time I got home an hour later with five sacks of groceries to put away, the mail had come. I *had* to take time to read the letters, and I couldn't resist looking at the new Sears catalog.

About 2:00, while we were eating lunch, some friends dropped by. "Since you are working now, you told us to come on a Saturday!"

I stuffed the unwashed clothes back into the hamper and pushed the vacuum sweeper to one side. Friends were more important than a few unwashed garments or a little dirt. But how I wished I had cleaned up the living room instead of looking at the catalog.

After they were gone and I had done the pile of dishes, there were still two loads of clothes to wash, beds to make, vacuuming, dusting and pressing. Mother called. My girlfriend called. The cat threw up.

As the sun began to set I put away the easel and closed the sewing machine.

While I made dinner the doorbell rang.

"Come in!" I yelled.

"I forgot to buy onions," my neighbor said as she again pushed aside a pile of dirty clothes. "Hey, I thought you said you were a fast worker."

"I don't know where the day has gone," I grumbled.

"There's still tomorrow."

"No there's not," I barked. "That's the Lord's day!"

"Do you have to go to church? I mean, you've got a good excuse to stay home."

"But I *want* to go!" I stormed.

Terrific testimony. I tried to smile. "I'll get all this done."

It was midnight when I crawled into bed. The laundry was done, the house was clean and part of Sunday's meal was prepared. But I felt robbed. Saturday, with all its golden hours, was gone.

And what had my neighbor thought of my display of temper?

27

Dear Father, please help me manage my time. The hours at home are so few. The hours of my life are so few. Help me not to waste them.

"You have made my days a mere handbreadth; the span of my years is as nothing before you. Each man's life is but a breath. Man is a mere phantom as he goes to and fro: He bustles about, but only in vain; he heaps up wealth, not knowing who will get it" (Psalm 39:5,6).

Breaking Bread

"Be sure to bring your lunch tomorrow," I reminded Alice on the way home from work Monday night. "It's Jim Jorgensen's first Bible class."

"That's right." She didn't sound very enthusiastic.

"You are planning to go, aren't you? I told him I thought there would be about seven of us."

"I'll go. But it's not my favorite way to spend a lunch hour."

At noon Tuesday, five of us were seated in Jim's office ready for him to begin. Every few seconds I looked at the door. I had hoped at least two more people would come, but they didn't. Jim seemed nervous as he moved things around on his desk.

"You ladies go right ahead and eat your lunch," he

said. "I'll talk while you eat."

Mitzi, being the tiniest, naturally was the one who brought the biggest lunch—turkey sandwich, Fritos, cookies and fruit. Marlene had a peanut butter sandwich and an apple; Beatrice Simpson had coffee and a cigarette.

"I'm always dieting," she explained with a tight smile. I was surprised to see Beatrice, even though she had noticed the Bible on my desk. I had the impression she was all business and not in the least interested in spiritual things. But here she was with a Bible in her hand.

Alice seemed agreeable as she ate her tuna salad sandwich. I slowly ate my favorite—yogurt.

"We're going to start with the Book of Romans," Jim announced. "This week I've been studying commentaries to see what I could say to you. In a way this is the hardest book in the Bible yet I believe we all need to understand it." He smiled at us.

Jim has the kind of smile that makes you feel as though you've been sprayed with sunshine. He looked down at his notes and reshuffled them.

"Romans is all about faith and justification. Do you all know what justification means? Some writer put it, '*just-as-if-I'd* never sinned.' In Romans we will learn that Jesus is the Justifier."

He smiled again and picked up his Bible. "So let's open our Bibles to Romans, chapter 1. That's in the New Testament."

There was a quick shuffle of paper sacks and Bibles. We looked up at him, waiting.

"I think we should pray," he said. He closed his Bible, folded his hands and closed his eyes. After a short but earnest appeal for the Lord to enable him

29

to teach, he opened his eyes and picked up the Bible again.

"I tell you," he said, shaking his head back and forth, "this is a heavy book." His hands trembled and I ached for him. Seeing how nervous he was made me nervous. After all, it was partly my fault.

"Dear Lord," I began to pray silently, "please, please help Jim get started." I was aware of restlessness in the room. Mitzi tapped her tiny foot; Marlene looked through her purse; Alice yawned.

"Lord, if he doesn't get started pretty soon they won't want to come next week," I prayed.

But Jim went on explaining what Romans was going to be about. When Beatrice looked at her watch I cleared my throat and he looked at me.

"How would it be, Jim, if you started reading?" I asked. "You could read a few verses, then explain them to us. And if we had questions we could ask them."

"Good idea!" He beamed at me. His eyes focused on the Bible. "Paul, a servant of Christ Jesus . . ."

At last! He was in gear. Now we would move ahead.

On the way home that night Alice said, "I thought the class was real interesting—after he got started. I'm looking forward to next week."

Somebody once said the Bible doesn't need to be defended—just declared.

Dear Lord, thank You for answering the prayer about Jim getting started. He is such a genuine Christian.

30

You're going to make him into a fine Bible teacher.

"Your word, O Lord, is eternal; it stands firm in the heavens. Your word is a lamp to my feet and a light for my path" (Psalm 119:89,105).

Whether We Live or Die

Yesterday Marlene Schultz invited me to lunch. She is a Senior Secretary who works for Richard Gallagher, the head of our department.

"I'm honored that you would ask me to lunch," I said as we sped along the freeway to some far-away restaurant.

"No, no," she said, her large, brown eyes almost stern. "I have an ulterior motive. I need to talk to you."

Her voice sounded strange and I looked over at her just as she glanced at me. There were tears in her eyes.

"You see, something happened to me awhile back," she began to explain, "and now I'm afraid—" She waved her hand as a signal she couldn't say any more. She swallowed and I looked at the freeway. We were passing cars right and left. I looked down at the speedometer and my stomach lurched. Now *I* was afraid.

"Marlene!" My voice sounded sharp. "Please don't cry now. You can't see through tears." Her mouth turned down and a big tear slid down her cheek.

"Please, Marlene, we don't have time to get in a wreck."

She tried to smile and blotted her eyes and nose. "Okay! No more tears."

She eased up on the gas, but we didn't talk any more for a few minutes. Evidently she couldn't talk about her fear objectively because she changed the subject.

"How do you like your job by now?" she asked.

"Fine. At first I didn't think I would ever catch on, but it's getting easier."

I turned in the seat so I could look at her. Marlene was tall and had a nice figure. She carried herself in a queenly way but I had noticed she wasn't the least snobbish; rather, she seemed to be exceptionally kind to everyone.

"How about you, Marlene? What's it like to work for Mr. Gallagher?"

"Hard! But he's a great boss. Even though he's younger than I, I really look up to him."

We didn't say much more until we were seated in an ornate, expensive restaurant. After we had ordered, she tried again.

"About four months ago Mama died." Her chin quivered.

Her make-up was flawless and her hair always had that "just done" look. It seemed odd for her to be talking about her "Mama" with tears in her eyes. This wasn't the same lady who gave us instructions. Tremulously, with much eye-wiping and nose-blowing, she continued.

"Mama's sister, my Aunt Clara, was my only remaining relative—and then she got sick." Marlene put her fist to her teeth, then took a deep breath.

"Aunt Clara became deathly ill. And then *I* got sick, really sick. So I promised God if He would let me live to take care of my aunt until she passed on I would be willing for Him to take me, too."

Her voice caught. "I said I'd be ready to go." Her eyes were brimming again. "So—Mama's sister died last month! And now God is ready to take me!"

She waved her hand again and looked away. Was Marlene afraid to die? Ever since I had accepted Christ as Savior I had said I wasn't afraid to die, but if it got right down to it, would I be? Marlene had invited me to lunch to comfort her. What could I say?

"Are you a Christian, Marlene?" What tact. What finesse.

"Of course. I've been a church member since I was seven."

"People can be church members and still not be Christians."

She looked pouty. "What do you mean?"

"A person has to accept Christ as payment for her sins. Have you ever done that?"

"Oh, that. Yes. When I was seven."

"You're sure?"

"It hurts my feelings for you to doubt me."

"Well, if you're sure then you have nothing to fear, even if you die. You'll be with the Lord."

"I know that." She lifted her chin slightly. "It's just that I don't want to leave my husband by himself." She picked up an olive, then put it down. "But I *promised* the Lord."

"Just because you told Him He could 'take' you, Marlene, doesn't mean He will! Remember, He's still calling the shots."

"I wish I could believe that," she said, like a child.

33

"Besides," I added, "if you die, who would ever take me to an elegant place like this again?"

We humans certainly worry about the dumbest things. It helps though to talk them over with a friend. I want to be Marlene's friend.

Dear Lord, help Marlene to stop being afraid and to trust You. Help me to help her. We both need You so much.

"If we live, we live to the Lord; and if we die, we die to the Lord. So, whether we live or die, we belong to the Lord" (Romans 14:8).

Poor Reception

Every day one of the secretaries has to take Mitzi's place out on the front desk while she has lunch. After I had been at Jenkins about three months Marlene said, "Okay, Mab. You know enough now to take your turn on the front desk. Go out there and let Mitzi teach you."

Mitzi's telephone instrument had thirty buttons on it.

"Good grief," I moaned. "I get mixed up with only four."

"You'll only have to answer this one," Mitzi said,

"except at noon."

"Noon? That's when I'll be out here."

"Oh, yeah. Well, don't worry. They hardly ever ring because everybody is out to lunch."

She picked up a clipboard with an application on it. "You'll have people come in at lunchtime to fill out an app, so give 'em one of these boards, okay? When they finish, you take the app off the board and put a new one on. Then you log the filled-out one."

"Log it?"

"Write it down. Here. On this chart."

The sheet she handed me had about ten columns to fill in. She took it away from me and pulled open a drawer.

"Be sure to have *nustars* fill out a W-4 form."

"Nustars?"

"New starts," she said sounding it out slowly. "New employees, okay?"

She gave me a quick glimpse of the W-4 forms in a drawer and banged it shut.

"If you need more apps they're in here; if you need to call a rep, the phone numbers are here. You may have to give a typing test, and the forms are here." In quick succession she opened and closed drawers. I nodded wisely, but when I returned to take her place at noon, I had already forgotten everything.

"I'll be back in one short hour," she boomed in her Amazon voice. "Toodle-doo."

Two people were in the room working on their applications, but the moment Mitzi left others came in—*and* the phone began to ring.

Lights indicated two lines were ringing at once and, just as I started to answer them, a sheriff in a crisp grey uniform and shining badge strode up to my desk. He said something about a summons and I panicked.

"There's no one here," I said quickly. "Everyone's at lunch until one and I don't work here."

He looked confused, took off his visored cap and scratched his head. He put his hat back on, looked at me threateningly and said, "I'll be back at one."

The telephone had never quit ringing and the lights now indicated five lines needed attention. Before I could decide which line to answer, the first two people in the room came to the desk with their finished applications. Several people now swarmed around the desk, all wanting applications. One trembling girl said she had an appointment for a typing test. And the phone kept ringing.

Calmly I began to push buttons. Each time I answered I murmured, "I'm sorry, there's no one here. Please call after one." Then I left the phone off the hook. I gave all the people applications to fill out, but I couldn't find the typing test. I think the girl was relieved. I know I was.

When Mitzi came back she boomed, "Any problems?"

I didn't look directly at her. "Not really."

"See? I told you it was easy."

As I went out the door on the way to the cafeteria I met the sheriff, but I walked on by as though I had never seen him before.

Every time I think I'm doing a pretty good job I produce evidence that proves I am *not*.

Dear Jesus, I confess my deceitfulness and my failure to be completely honest. Help me do a better job next time I'm on the front desk.

"Humble yourselves before the Lord, and he will lift you up" (James 4:10).

A New Dress for the Old Cross

"Want to see my Easter outfit?" Sharon asked breathlessly one day after lunch. She opened a bag from an exclusive shop and took out an exquisite soft blue dress.

"Oh, Sharon! The color is perfect for you."

"You should see it on! It's like it was made for me. Look at the shoes!" She opened another bag and took out a shoe box, then put on a pair of white, high-heeled sandals and twirled around. "And there's a purse to match. See?"

I felt a surge of jealousy, but only for a moment. My husband and I had some goals to reach. Clothes could come later.

"Where are you going to wear the outfit?" I asked.

"To my mom's. The whole family will be there for dinner." She examined a seam carefully. "What are you going to do?"

"Go to church and then have dinner with my mother."

"What are you wearing?"

"Probably that peach colored dress I wore the first day. It's still pretty. Anyway," I swallowed hard, "clothes for Easter aren't as important when you get older."

"You're probably right," Sharon said as she held the dress up and twisted back and forth. "I guess Easter is just another day. Wonder where the idea of getting new clothes for Easter came from?"

"I read once that it's because Easter is a celebration of the fact that Jesus Christ came back to life after He was crucified. Everyone was so glad they wanted to put on their best things—like for a party."

Sharon had unbuckled her sandals and was putting them away, so I couldn't see her face.

"Then too, our pastor said it's symbolic of putting on new life. If you accept Christ as your Savior you exchange your old life for a new life."

Sharon straightened up and looked at me with round eyes. Her face was pink. "Personally, I don't see anything wrong with *this* life." She folded the new dress and slid it back into the sack.

"I like this life too, but—I don't explain it very well," I apologized. "Do you think that maybe you and Mark could come with us to church Easter? Anyway, you've got to show off that new outfit!"

"Oh, I'm sorry, Mab," she said too quickly, "but I've got to help my mom get dinner." She flashed her generous smile. "But sometime maybe I will."

How can I show her that new clothes for Easter aren't nearly as important as Easter?

Lord, I'm trying to be a witness, but why am I so powerless?

"Do your best to present yourself to God as one approved, a workman who does not need to be ashamed and who correctly handles the word of truth" (II Timothy 2:15).

"Therefore, if anyone is in Christ, he is a new creation; the old has gone, the new has come!" (II Corinthians 5:17).

Rookie Recruiter

Yesterday I had barely taken off the typewriter cover when Mr. Larson called in.

"My wife is very sick," he said. "I'm going to stay home with her."

"Oh, I'm sorry," I said. "I'll pray for her." The second I said it I wished I hadn't. Mr. Larson had let me know that he most definitely was not interested in religion. I was usually careful not to antagonize him but the offer to pray had just popped out. He ignored it and began to give me lengthy, detailed instructions about work.

When I hung up I felt as though I had been let out of school. I was sorry for his wife and I did pray for her, but it would be great not to have him going through the applications on my desk, asking if I had remembered to do such and such.

I didn't dislike Howard Larson, and I respected his ability, but he made me nervous. In all fairness to him, I'm sure I made him nervous also!

About nine o'clock Ann Valdemar, one of the wheels up in Cost Planning, called. I was about half-afraid of Ann. Austere, beautiful, and competent, she didn't give a blink of her eye what anyone thought of her. Mr. Larson was terrified of her.

"Don't ever cross her," he had once warned. "She has power and she could get you fired."

"Isn't Howard there?" she asked accusingly.

"I'm sorry, Ann" (she had insisted on first names when we were first introduced), "but Mr. Larson, uh, Howard's wife is si—uh, ill, and he won't be in."

"Drat! He promised me some engineers this morning."

"Oh, really? What were their names?"

"How do I know?" she retorted. "I've never seen the applications."

"Oh! I see. You mean Howard promised to get some applications up to you?"

"Now you've got it, sweetie. What did you think I meant?"

"Brain's not engaged as usual," I mumbled. I cleared my throat. "I'll go through his desk, Ann, and bring you any engineer applications or resumes I find. Okay?"

"Please." Click.

Perspiring, I hurried into Mr. Larson's office and began to go through the stacks of applications piled on his desk. I wasn't qualified for this. It took years of training to know what experience and education was required for certain openings.

"Oh, Lord, please help me find the right ones. I

need You!"

I selected five applications that looked okay to me and hurried up to the tenth floor. Ann seemed pleased, and when I turned to go she said, "Let's have lunch sometime."

Wow! I ran giddily down the stairs. Wow!

This morning when I told Mr. Larson about the applications I thought he was going to burst into tears.

"You should never have done that! Now she'll have us for sure!"

"But what could I do?" I snapped back. "She demanded applications. I had to take her something!"

"Don't you see?" he cried, as he unfurled his handkerchief and blotted his balding head. "You couldn't possibly have known if those were qualified applicants. Before I *ever* send any application up to her I go over and over it—the education, the experience, the age, everything—so she won't find fault. Now she'll have another complaint about Personnel. If only you had called me!" He slumped at his desk and I crept to mine.

As I sat down, Cara, Ann's secretary, handed the applications to me. A note was attached: "These look good. Invite for interview."

I took them in to Howard and slapped them on the desk.

"We lucked out," he said.

"Would you believe—oh, never mind." I bit my lip.

"What?" He looked up at me expectantly. "What were you going to say?"

"I prayed I would choose the right ones." I almost ran to my desk.

He think's I'm foolish anyway—might as well be a

fool for Christ.

Thank You, Lord! I know it was Your wisdom yester-day that chose those applications. How great You are, and how kind You are to me!

"Oh, the depth of the riches of the wisdom and knowledge of God! How unsearchable his judgments, and his paths beyond tracing out!" (Romans 11:33).

The Morning Star

"Did you know Mr. Dudley is leaving?" Sharon asked one morning.

"No! I thought he was making Personnel his career."

"He is, but he's going to another company."

"That's a shame. When is he leaving?"

"Next week," Sharon said morosely. "I hate for him to go. He's such a neat boss. Wonder who will take his place?"

I hated for him to leave, too. Not because he was a neat boss, but because I had never had the nerve to talk to him about his soul. The fact that he was so deep into astrology had intimidated me. I wondered now if his horoscope had told him to move on.

One thing was certain. Only the Morning Star could save him and somehow I was going to have to tell him. But how? The only thing we had in common was we both liked yogurt.

The next morning I took him a carton of my favorite, caramel-pecan yogurt.

"How did you know I didn't have time for breakfast?" he beamed as he reached for it.

"Maybe the stars?" I said and immediately regretted it. Why do I say such stupid things?

Mr. Dudley was already wolfing it down.

"Mmm! Good!" he murmured. "Of course it was the stars. My horoscope for today said I would have affirmative encounters."

"Mr. Dudley, uh—that's what I wanted to talk to you about."

"Your horoscope?" He turned around in his swivel chair and reached toward the bookcase. "Have a book right here."

"No, no. See, I—" I could feel my face get red. "What I'm trying to say is, I don't believe in that. If you want to, of course that's your business, but I believe in Jesus Christ and I've put my trust in Him, and He knows my future, and so I don't. I mean, I don't have to. Know the future, I mean . . ."

He quit eating. With his spoon held up in the air, he looked at me. After a second or two he put his spoon down.

"I accepted Christ when I was a little boy," he said.

I gasped with relief. "You did?"

He nodded. Suddenly his eyes looked moist.

"Well, don't be offended, but why do you believe in that?" I pointed at the book with astrological signs on it.

"Why not? Didn't God make the stars?"

43

"Yes. That's just it. He made *them*. So what do *they* know?"

He looked thoughtful. "You have a point."

His telephone rang and I waved goodbye.

On his last day while he was saying his goodbyes, he came to me. "You're a nice lady. Pray for me."

What a relief to find out Mr. Dudley is a Christian. What a shame I didn't talk to him sooner.

Dear Lord, give me more courage to talk about You. And help Mr. Dudley to quit looking to the stars, but to look only to the Morning Star—You.

"Let your astrologers come forward, those star-gazers who make predictions month by month, let them save you from what is coming upon you. Surely they are like stubble; the fire will burn them up. They cannot even save themselves from the power of the flame" (Isaiah 47:13b,14a).

" 'I, Jesus, have sent my angel to give you this testimony for the churches. I am the Root and the Offspring of David, and the bright Morning Star' " (Revelation 22:16).

Noon Buffoon

"Want to go shopping with us during lunch hour?" Glenna asked. "Bonnie, Evelyn and I are going to the Sampler."

"Sure!" I was glad for the opportunity to get acquainted with them, and I had also heard of the fantastic discounts at the Sampler. "The only thing is, I usually eat with Alice."

"Bring her too," Glenna said. "There's plenty of room."

"You'll love the Sampler," Evelyn added. "I get most of my clothes there."

When we got there I was amazed. There must have been thousands of garments of every kind—pantsuits, dresses in all lengths, blouses, sweaters, separates. There was an abundance of everything women wear.

Bonnie, a beautiful former model, began to fan through the pantsuits.

"Only seventeen dollars!" she exclaimed. Every so often she would take a hanger off the rack and put the garment over her arm. Suddenly she disappeared into one of the dressing rooms.

Alice oohed and aahed the dresses. With an armload of blouses, Glenna also disappeared. Evelyn had slacks and sweaters with her as she headed for the dressing rooms. I kept running from one area to another.

"Lunch hour will be over," I moaned, and grabbed a couple of pantsuits to try on.

Alone in my cubicle I was aware of my failure to stay on the protein diet. I couldn't get the zipper up on either pair of pants. While I put on my clothes I could hear bits of conversation:

"This is beautiful!"

"I think I'll get this."

Frantic for fear I'd miss out, I slapped my way through a blouse rack.

"I've got to buy something," I mumbled. But the blouses I liked were three times what I could pay. I began to look at the tags first and found one that had been marked down from $22.00 to $5.00. It was striped pink, orange and gray, with red zits all over it. It was the ugliest print I had ever seen, but if it had once been $22.00 couldn't I learn to like it?

At the counter all the girls were standing around looking at their watches. The lunch hour was gone.

In the car I said, "Let's see what you bought."

No one had bought anything.

"But I thought you said you got most of your clothes there," I said to Evelyn.

"I do. But I come on Saturday and take my time."

"Me too," Bonnie added. "I've learned if I buy in a hurry I usually regret it."

I covertly peeked into my sack. I think she's right.

I wonder if Mother would like a striped blouse for her birthday?

Dear Lord, I've just thrown away part of my wages on a dumb thing I'll never wear. Forgive me for being more influenced by others than by You.

"The plans of the diligent lead to profit as surely as haste leads to poverty" (Proverbs 21:5).

Bug Off

Day before yesterday as I watched Sharon type I was suddenly touched with tenderness. She's so young, I thought, so pretty—so lost. Why couldn't I make myself witness to her? True, I had invited her to church but I was too cowardly to tell her she was a sinner and that Christ had died for her.

"Yes, but the Bible says to be ready to give an answer to everyone who *asks*," I argued to myself. "Sharon has never asked me anything about my faith."

"But it also says to 'preach the word ... in season and out of season; correct, rebuke and encourage,' " I said back to myself. "You're not doing your job."

Impulsively I scooted my chair close. "Sharon?"

She stopped typing and looked at me with her baby doll eyes.

"What's up?" she squeaked.

"I was just wondering." I could feel my courage seeping away. "How about going to Bible class with me Tuesday? Jim is—"

"No thanks." She turned back to her typewriter without her usual smile. "Sorry, but religion just isn't my bag."

My face got hot and I felt ashamed. Why did *I* feel ashamed? Because she thought she didn't need God? It made me angry. *Lord, I'm not going to try to witness to her again!*

"*Try loving her,*" He seemed to say.

So yesterday I bought a plant for her desk, and so she wouldn't be suspicious I also bought one for myself. She was pleased and thanked me several times.

47

"Let's have lunch together," she said, mid-morning. "I know a great Mexican restaurant."

It's working! I thought.

During lunch I encouraged her to talk about herself. Her goals in life were to buy more furniture, a better home and "a car bigger than my Volksie."

"How about children?" I asked.

"Maybe. But not until I get all the things I want."

As I listened to her talk I promised the Lord if she asked me anything about myself I would tell her about Jesus. But she never did.

We prayed for her last night during devotions, and then I went through my tracts to see if there was one she might read. I chose a colorful one with a picture of a little car going over a hill.

This morning she brought adorable ceramic flower pots for our plants. After we had repotted them, cleaned up the soil mix and were just sitting there admiring our plants, I took out the tract and said, "Sharon, I know religion isn't your bag and I'm not trying to make you uncomfortable. But the message in this little pamphlet is good. Please read it and see what you think."

Her eyes grew even larger and showed hostility.

"Sharon, I promise you, unless you want to talk about it I won't bring it up again, okay?" I gave her the tract.

She smiled when she looked at it.

"How darling! It looks just like my Volksie!" She zipped off a piece of scotch tape and without even opening the tract, stuck it up by her "BUG OFF" sign.

Sharon, you out-foxed me. Or did you? At least the

tract is in your possession.

Dear Lord, she's got the gospel message. Please use it for Your glory.

"As the rain and the snow come down from heaven, and do not return to it without watering the earth and making it bud and flourish, so that it yields seed for the sower and bread for the eater, so is my word that goes out from my mouth: It will not return to me empty, but will accomplish what I desire and achieve the purpose for which I sent it" (Isaiah 55:10,11).

Count the Cost

"Did you know Don Braddock is leaving?" Howard asked me one morning.

"Really? Why?"

"He's going back up to Engineering. He was only here on a training basis."

"He isn't a regular recruiter?"

"No, he was here to learn Personnel problems. He's from Petro-Chemical. He's a civil engineer."

Howard put his hands in his pockets and swayed back and forth on his heels. "He's leaving next week and they'll send another man down to learn."

"Is he going to have a farewell luncheon?"

"I don't know about that. Usually the secretaries

49

plan those things and Don was never assigned a regular secretary."

"He's an awfully nice fellow. It would be a shame for us to ignore him. I think I'll talk to Marlene."

"I don't know," Marlene said brightly. "I don't think anyone wants to take the responsibility."

"Well, I'll do it," I said. "He's too nice not to have a luncheon."

"It isn't hard," Marlene said. "You decide where you want to have the luncheon, call them for reservations, find out what they serve, and how much it costs. Then send a bulletin around for people to sign up."

She batted her eyelashes confidentially. "Easy."

Sharon suggested the country club because they would add everything on one bill. The nice hostess at the country club told me, "Our buffet is $2.75 per person, which includes coffee or tea, and I suggest you collect from everyone before you come."

Twenty-four people signed the bulletin and put their money in the envelope. I was awfully nervous about having $66.00 of other people's money in my purse.

We had a wonderful lunch, Don gave a speech, and Mr. Gallagher complimented me on engineering the luncheon. I was having fun until the waitress gave me a check for $79.00. That was $13.00 more than I had collected.

"Is something wrong?" Marlene asked when I choked.

I waved her off and gave her a big smile. "Get us some more coffee while I go up and pay the check."

The cashier went over the bill:

	24 people	X	$ 2.75	=	$66.00
plus	Don's lunch		2.75	=	68.75
plus	15% Tip		10.30	=	$79.00

"I was so glad I had our checkbook," I told my husband that night.

"Didn't you tell anybody?" he asked.

"I was too ashamed for being such a dumbbell."

"You *are* a dumbbell for not telling them. If each person would just give their tip of forty cents it would help a lot. I think you should tell them. Thirteen dollars is a lot of money."

Groan. Sigh. Maybe the Lord will come tonight.

I'll have to tell them tomorrow even if it hurts my pride. Being stupid once is bad enough.

Dear Lord, again I ask You to forgive me for trying to appear wiser than I am. It's pride. Help me tomorrow to admit I made a mistake so I can collect what is due me.

"When pride comes, then comes disgrace, but with humility comes wisdom" (Proverbs 11:2).

Car Sick

We're not supposed to attach human characteristics to inanimate objects but sometimes I think my car hates me, and tonight I hate him. (Bobbie pointed out that since men call their vehicles "she" it's only fitting that we call ours "*he*.")

He's a 1971 Ford LTD. And that's one of the things I have against him. I've never been able to find out what LTD stands for. I have asked several people, including an engineer, but no one knows for sure. One person said he thought it stood for limited.

"There are a limited number of them," he explained. But that couldn't be it. There are at least two on every block. I think it stands for Large Tin Disaster.

When we first bought it I drove it for two years with no trouble, but now that I have started to work—and especially since Alice and I share a ride— it has been one repair bill after another. So far I've spent $116.00 on him, not counting his gasoline and oil.

The first thing was a new battery. The only batteries I've ever bought were for my tape recorder, so I almost had a nosebleed when the mechanic said, "$40.00." But it was great to have the engine start with the first flip of the key.

However, it wasn't long until he began to choke, snort and stall. All his horses wanted to come in last. It was not only embarrassing to creep along the freeway at 22 miles per hour during peak hours but it was terrifying.

"I think every driver should see to it that his car is in good condition," Alice said, gripping her purse and bracing her feet. "Especially if he's going to have riders."

I took him in that Saturday for a physical, or whatever they do. I couldn't make out all the blue carbon scribbling, but I could plainly read, *$51.00.*

Yesterday after work the starter groaned, then wouldn't make another sound. The man in the tow truck got it started, then told me, "It needs a bendix spring."

"He's crazy," my husband said last night after LTD started twenty-five consecutive times.

"*I'm* crazy," I thought as I telephoned Alice to come and get me this morning.

Tonight while eating dinner we talked about trading him for a new, smaller car, one that would get better mileage. But as I looked at him there in the driveway he looked magnificent. He has a gorgeous body and we've covered a lot of miles together. My throat tightened.

"Never fear, Ford dear," I whispered. I blew him a kiss. "We can still run around together."

I can get a lot of repairs for the price of a new car. After all, a car is just transportation.

Thank You, dear Lord for my car. What a privilege it is to own a car, to have it paid for, and to be able to drive.

". . . always giving thanks to God the Father for everything, in the name of our Lord Jesus Christ" (Ephesians 5:20).

In the Book

"Here's your new phone book," Marlene said. She had an armful of yellow, plastic-covered directories.

"Wonder if my name is in this one."

I thought back to the first week I had been at the John R. Jenkins Company. I had gone up to the second floor to see Alice. She looked up from her work, her eyes wide with surprise.

"What are you doing up here this time of day?"

"I wanted to tell you I can't have lunch with you. I have an appointment with the eye doctor."

"Why didn't you just call me?"

I grinned, embarrassed. "I forgot your extension."

"Why didn't you look in the company phone book?"

"I guess I didn't think of it. Is your name in it?"

She reached for the directory, opened it and pointed to her name.

I took it out of her hand and flipped through it.

"Sure a lot of names," I commented.

"About five thousand," Alice said. "Your name will be in it next time. They print new ones every six months."

And now it had been six months.

I opened the new book quickly. "Yep! There am I!"

Marlene smiled happily.

"Doesn't that make you feel secure?" she said.

"Yes! Almost as secure as having my name in the Lamb's Book of Life."

"What did you say?"

"The Lamb's Book—you know, God's book. The Book of Life."

"Oh. That book." She looked troubled. "I hope my

name is in it."

"Marlene, you've accepted Christ. You know it is."

She smiled wistfully. "I surely hope so. I try to be a good girl."

"It's not by works, Marlene. You know that from what Jim is teaching in Romans."

She nodded vaguely.

At home that evening I told my husband how exasperated I was with Marlene for being a doubter and with myself for not knowing the Bible better.

"There are all kinds of Bible verses on eternal security," I said. "We need to dig them out and memorize them."

"Sometimes I have doubts," my husband said. "We do need to study more."

After dinner we got out the concordance and the Bible and wrote down a lot of scripture references: John 3:36, John 5:24, John 10:9, Galatians 2:16, I John 5:13.

"I'm going to go in early in the morning and type these," I said. "I'll give them to Marlene and keep a copy for us."

"We ought to make an effort to memorize them," my husband said.

The next day when I gave Marlene the sheet of Bible verses I said, "By the time we memorize these, we'll *know* our names are in the Book of Life."

"I *hope* so," Marlene said, and put the paper in her purse.

My name is in the company directory because I am an employee. My name is in the Lamb's Book of Life because I am a member of God's family through Jesus Christ.

Dear Lord, I thank You that I've worked long enough to have my name in the company directory but, oh, how I thank You for putting my name in Your Book of Life.

". . . I will never erase his name from the book of life . . ." (Revelation 3:5).

"Nothing impure will ever enter it . . . but only those whose names are written in the Lamb's book of life" (Revelation 21:27).

"Whosoever believes in the Son has eternal life, but whoever rejects the Son will not see life, for God's wrath remains on him" (John 3:36).

"I write these things to you who believe in the name of the Son of God so that you may know that you have eternal life" (I John 5:13).

Mouse In-House

One morning when I got to my desk there was a teaspoon of dirt on it. I looked up but there was nothing wrong with the ceiling. I couldn't figure it out.

"Was there an earthquake?" I called out to Bertha, who is always the first one to arrive in the department.

"Not that I know of," she answered. She turned off her typewriter and walked the two rows to my desk. "Why?"

"Look at my desk."

Her round eyes got rounder as she bent her mini-braided head for a closer look. Finally she leaned back and began to laugh. When Bertha laughed her whole body shook and you could hear her all over the room.

"Looks to me like the earthquake was the clean-up crew. I guess they knocked your plant over."

"Of course. That's what it is."

"Right!" she chuckled musically.

The next morning my desk had dirt on it again, and this time the flowerpot was on its side.

"What's the matter with those clumsy guys?" I grumbled to Sharon and Judy. Judy Smith is a new secretary, and she and Sharon have been having coffee together each morning.

"How come they haven't knocked over your flowerpot, Sharon?" I asked as I began to clean up the mess.

"Probably because it wasn't in my horoscope," Sharon teased.

As I brushed at the dirt I recognized a tiny mouse calling card.

"Aha!" I pointed at the evidence. "Tomorrow I'll get a mousetrap."

"Oh, you wouldn't kill it!" Sharon cried in her baby voice.

"Oh, no!" Judy also wailed.

"Of course I will," I said. "Mice are disease carriers."

"But what if he's somebody reincarnated," Judy moaned.

I looked at her. Her brown eyes were full of anguish.

"You're serious!" I said.

"My boyfriend is studying Eastern religions," she went on, "and he said that Hindus won't even kill a fly for fear it might be a relative."

I sprayed Fantastic on my desk. "That's baloney," I said as I rubbed.

"But how do you *know*?" Judy asked. "My boyfriend says that we all keep coming back in different forms until we're perfected and then we're absorbed by Nirvana, or something like that."

"The Bible says when we die we go directly to heaven—that is, if we believe in Jesus."

Judy stared at me and my words sounded immature, even to me. "There's none of that in-between stuff!"

"Can you show me in the Bible where it says that?" she asked.

"Sure," I said and reached for the Bible. I began to turn pages. Where was that passage?

"Oh, come on, Judy," Sharon whined. "We won't have time to get coffee."

Judy began to walk away. She called over her shoulder, "I want to see it sometime, okay?"

Whew! Thank the Lord I'll have a chance to look up the right scriptures.

Lord Jesus, it is exciting to have the opportunity to talk to Judy about You. Please don't let her fall for that reincarnation stuff.

"We are confident, I say, and would prefer to be away from the body and at home with the Lord" (II Corinthians 5:8).

Executrix

When I came in this morning both mousetraps had done their grim job. The trap on the desk next to the plant had a tiny mouse in it, no longer than an inch and a half not counting the tail. The other trap on the floor under the desk had the granddaddy of them all. He was at least twice as big as the other one.

Maybe it is because my parents were farmers and have always taken it as a matter course that "varmints" had to be done away with, but I didn't feel sad or repulsed as I picked up the traps. I didn't feel anything except relieved that my plant wouldn't be used as a litter box anymore. I was trying to decide if I should empty the traps into my wastebasket or dump them in the big can out in the lobby when Judy and Sharon walked up.

"Oh, my——!" Sharon cried. She clapped a hand over her mouth.

"You've killed them!" Judy screamed. She bent down for a closer look. I restrained the impulse to scare her with them. "Oh, look at his poor little eyes! They're open! Look at his fur—"

"What are you guys screaming about?" Mitzi boomed from the door.

"Mab murdered some mice!" Sharon called out.

"Look at their darling pink feet," Judy said. "Oh, I'm sure this was some little girl somewhere."

"How awful," someone said. There were several people now grouped around the little corpses. Even Mr. Wright, the Division Manager, dashed over for a quick look.

"Little devils. They never had a chance did they?"

"Hey, Mab," Bonnie said reproachfully, "I thought you were a nice lady."

"Yeah—how could you do that?" Glenna chimed.

Suddenly I felt like some kind of monster.

"Good grief!" I yelped. "They're only mice." No one smiled. Everyone looked either sad or horrified. I couldn't believe it.

"*Dirty* mice," I added.

"But they were alive," Judy said with a catch in her voice.

Gustav Brit, the engineer who had taken Don Braddock's place, was the only one who was smiling.

"Give them to me," he said with a wicked look. "I'll give them a nice funeral. I'll put them in an envelope and send them up to the Building Engineer!"

I was the only one who laughed. They walked away slowly, as people do at a cemetery.

Death is awesome, somber. Even little dead mice

60

bring dread and fear to these people. How could they be so concerned about the death of two mice, yet not seem to have any concern for *their* eternal lives?

Lord, I want to show them the love of Jesus. Please don't let them think I'm cruel.

" 'Of the animals that move about on the ground, these are unclean for you: the weasel, the rat, any kind of great lizard' " (Leviticus 11:29).

"Do not be afraid of those who kill the body but cannot kill the soul. Rather, be afraid of the one who can destroy both soul and body in hell" (Matthew 10:28).

Neat Feat

"Can you do some work for me today?" Ralph Barns, one of the recruiters, asked. "Glenna just called in sick and I have some stuff that has to go out today."

Howard said it would be okay, so I went over to Glenna's desk to do Ralph's work. When I sat down and opened one of the drawers, I gasped. The file folders stood at military attention, every label perfectly typed. I felt the color rise on my neck as I thought of my file drawer with its bulging, beat-up folders, some identified in felt-tip scrawl, some with labels, some nameless. What if the situation was reversed, I was sick, and Glenna was at my desk? I couldn't stand the thought.

Carefully I opened the top drawer. It looked like an ad for a desk company. Not only was every pen, pencil and eraser in its place, even the paper clips lay side by side like cribs in a nursery. How could anybody be that neat?

Other drawers displayed company envelopes in tight groups, and all the stationery from letterheads to carbon sets were in precise order. The shelf above her desk held the notebook binders, each the same distance from the edge of the shelf with typed labels placed exactly the same distance from the top of the binder.

The desk itself was immaculate. Even the leaves on her ivy plant were evenly divided on two stems. Nobody could be this neat. She must have known she was going to be sick and cleaned it up last night. But a luncheon was planned for today and Glenna loved to eat. She wouldn't be absent unless she was really sick. But how could anybody work in this showcase? *I couldn't.*

I took Ralph's work back to my desk but I couldn't concentrate too well when I looked around at the disgusting disarray. My top drawer didn't have neat rows of pens and pencils; it had rows of wadded up Kleenex, candy, cookies and tangled paper clips. Even my Charlie plant looked disorderly with his fallen leaves and scraggly stems. Poor fellow. Probably the reason he looked so bad was because every time I reached for the dictionary, Company Policy fell down on him.

Something would have to be done, I thought,

ashamed. Glumly I took some forms out to Mitzi, and my spirits lifted quite a bit when I saw a new sign on her desk:

"A NEAT DESK IS A SIGN OF A SICK MIND."

"That's the greatest thing I've ever read," I told her.

However, when I finish Ralph's work I am going to clean up my desk. The possibility of being sick and having someone else in my place worries me.

I wonder if I'll ever learn that I don't really save time by doing things half-way *now,* with the promise to do them right *later.*

Dear Jesus, I know that the 'gospel according to me' will be the only Bible some of these employees ever read. Help me not only to do a good job, but also to be as neat as Glenna.

"And whatever you do, whether in word or deed, do it all in the name of the Lord Jesus, giving thanks to God the Father through him" (Colossians 3:17).

Retirement Plan

I feel sad today.

A couple of weeks ago Sharon confided that at noon she was going on a job interview at a loan company.

"Since Mr. Dudley quit they keep farming me out like I'm in a steno pool. I hate my job."

"But aren't they trying to find a replacement for Mr. Dudley?" I asked.

"They say they are, but you see what they're doing. Mr. Larson is doing some of his work and Bobbie is doing the rest. Bobbie has Louise and Mr. Larson has you."

Her wide, blue eyes narrowed and her mouth turned down. "They don't need me—and I don't need them!"

"Sharon, don't make any quick moves. Are you sure you've thought it through? We've got life insurance here, and medical, and retirement."

"Retirement? Who cares? My husband has a retirement plan with his company. Anyway, I'm too young to worry about insurance and all that stuff. The future will take care of itself."

That day Sharon came in from lunch ten minutes late. Her blond hair was a little windblown and her cheeks were pink from running, but her eyes were sparkling.

"I got the job," she whispered. "I'm going to make a hundred dollars *more* a month!"

"A hundred dollars!" I repeated.

"And you know what else?" Her mouth was in such a wide grin she could hardly talk. "I'm going to be the secretary to the manager of the office!"

"Man—" I said in awe. I was older than Sharon. I was sure we made about the same salary, and now she not only would be earning a hundred a month more, but she would have "prestige" as well. Maybe *I* should look for a better job.

"What about medical and retirement?" I asked.
She waved her hand and wrinkled her nose.
"No—it's not a big company. But I told you. The future doesn't matter. Just think how much sooner I can get my furniture and car!"

Today we gave Sharon a wonderful send-off. Everybody either brought her goodies or a gift and we had lunch at her favorite restaurant. I'm really going to miss Sharon. I almost cried when she packed up all her things. I watched her as she took down her pictures and signs. She threw a lot of the things away, but the tract with the little car on it went into her purse.

Maybe she isn't concerned about the future right now, either in life or death, but I'm glad she saved that gospel message.

I may never see Sharon again on this earth. But I believe I was put beside her for the purpose of telling her about Christ. I'm sure I'll see her "over there."

Dear Lord, I've planted the seed. Someone else will water it. I know You will make it grow.

"Still others, like seed sown among thorns, hear the word; but the worries of this life, the deceitfulness of wealth and the desires for other things come in and choke the word, making it unfruitful. Others, like seed sown on good soil, hear the word, accept it . . ." (Mark 4:18-20).

He Knows My Name!

Yesterday all of us got a memo from Gene Wright, the division head, requesting that we attend a staff meeting in the big conference room. I was excited because, although I had been to several staff meetings in our own Employment Section, I had never attended one where all of Personnel would be there.

Mr. Wright is about thirty-six, very good looking and a dynamo. He never seems to walk anywhere. He moves like the road-runner—W-H-I-Z-Z. He has never spoken to me outside of his comments over the dead mice, so I didn't know whether or not I liked him until he opened the meeting. He was witty, funny, yet so humble.

"I wonder if you have any idea how many people we have hired since I came to work here five years ago? It's in the thousands! And you, my personnel family, have done all the work."

He told several jokes (some were not nice), then he explained why he had called the meeting.

No. 1—He was going to our branch in Saudi Arabia for two years to handle Personnel at the site.

No. 2—He wanted to introduce John Burgemeir, the man who would take Mr. Dudley's place.

"John is not only going to be hiring," Mr. Wright said, "but he is going to introduce a new service here at Jenkins—'Job Posting.' I'm going to let John explain it to you himself."

John Burgemeir was about five foot eleven, stocky but not fat. He had blond hair, styled with a part on

66

the side. He looked like the models for Father's Day presents—good looking yet homey.

He explained the new service and though it sounded complicated it boiled down to the fact that every opening in the company would be posted on various bulletin boards throughout the company, so present employees would have a chance at the job before strangers were hired.

Later in the day Dick Gallagher brought John through our department and introduced him to each one of us. He seemed as relaxed as a relative, and I liked him.

This morning when I came to work I was surprised to see John already at work in Mr. Dudley's old office. He had moved in and set pictures of his wife and son on his desk.

He looked up with a smile. "Good morning, Mab."

I was shocked! He remembered my name.

Sharon, I think you quit too soon.

Dear Lord, help me to remember names. What a good way to start a friendly relationship. It means a lot in this busy world for a stranger to remember your name. But how much more amazing it is that You know everyone's name!

". . . You have said, 'I know you by name . . .' " (Exodus 33:12b).

". . . so that you may know that I am the Lord . . . who calls you by name" (Isaiah 45:3b).

Room at the Top

I was hard at work on some forms that had to be in Records by lunchtime. I didn't realize Marlene was introducing a new girl in the department until they stood between Sharon's old desk and me.

"This is Christy," Marlene said, smiling benevolently. "Christy Moon."

I looked up at a thin, beautiful black girl, probably twenty-two.

"She's going to be your new side-kick."

Christy winced at the term.

"Space-mate sounds better, Marlene," I said and smiled. "Hi, Christy. It will be good to have someone beside me again."

She nodded politely.

"You're John Burgemeir's new secretary?"

"Assistant," she corrected. She raised her eyebrows slightly. She shrugged the strap of a huge canvas bag off her shoulder and put it on the desk. "There is a difference."

I looked up at Marlene. She smiled and nodded.

"The last I heard he was going to get a secretary," I said.

"I will be working closely with John on the new program," Christy said, "but I am not a secretary." She smiled at me kindly, as though I were a child who had gotten mixed up as to which shoe to put on.

"Whatever! It's good to have you."

"I'll leave you now, Christy," Marlene said and patted her shoulder. "You're in good hands."

I looked up at the clock.

"I'll be glad to help you with anything I can, Christy, after I get these done. The pressure here is unbelievable some days, and this is one of those days."

She waved her hand and shook her head. "No problem." She dug around in her purse. "Can we smoke?"

Disappointment. Sharon and I had often discussed our good fortune that neither of us smoked.

"Sure." She already had a long slender cigarette between her lips, ready to light.

"Ashtray?" she asked. Her cigarette bobbed up and down as she spoke.

"I'll see if I can find one, but could you use the saucer under my plant until I can get one?"

I banged away at my work with an occasional glance at Christy. She was getting settled at her new desk, and when our eyes met she smiled stiffly. Everything was ready for Howard's signature at ten minutes before twelve.

"Do you have lunch plans, Christy?"

"No." Her voice was soft and cultured.

"Would you like to go to the cafeteria with me?"

She nodded.

On our way to the cafeteria I realized she was taller than I, which would make her about five seven. I also noticed that the men, both white and black, eyed her appreciatively.

At lunch, by asking a lot of questions I learned she was divorced and had a little boy not quite two. Could the attitude I had mistaken for sophisticated snobbery be only a garment put on by a little girl to keep from falling apart?

But any attempt to sympathize was rejected.

"I brought it on myself," she said. "I can cope."

We worked on our salads for a few moments.

"So what have you got against secretaries?" I

asked abruptly. The question seemed to startle her, then she broke up. She was even prettier when she laughed.

"Between you and me, I haven't got the skills! Besides, I couldn't stand to be a paper shuffler." She lit one of her long slender cigarettes. "If I am going to work, then I am going to the top."

Lady, you sound as though you know what you want. I may wind up working for you.

Dear Lord, Christy makes me feel ill at ease. And I don't like the smoke. But I believe You put her beside me. Help me to like her and make me brave enough to tell her about Jesus.

"Now listen, you who say, 'Today or tomorrow we will go to this or that city, spend a year there, carry on business and make money.' Why, you do not even know what will happen tomorrow. What is your life? You are a mist that appears for a little while and then vanishes. Instead, you ought to say, 'If it is the Lord's will, we will live and do this or that.' As it is, you boast and brag. All such boasting is evil" (James 4:13-16).

Cowardly Christian

We said goodbye to Gene Wright this morning. It was pretty sad. Some of the older women who had known him for a long time cried. I saw one man put his arm around Mr. Wright's shoulder as he shook hands.

"He leaves here at two o'clock," Howard sighed. "He'll be in Saudi this time tomorrow."

"Isn't it dangerous over there?" I asked.

"You bet it is. But the company needs him. *C'est le guerre.*"

Mr. Wright was working his way slowly through the department, shaking hands, kissing, talking. As he came nearer to my desk I thought: *What if he never comes back? I have never told him how to be saved. But he is the head of this department. Anyway, it's too late now. Isn't it?*

Frantically I looked through my purse for an appropriate tract. (How thankful I am for a church with a huge tract rack.) As though the Lord had put it there, I found one with a picture of an airplane on the cover. I folded it into a tiny square. Mr. Wright was at my desk!

"Mab, I'm sorry I haven't had a chance to know you better." His brown eyes were more sparkly than ever.

"Me too, Mr. Wright."

He put out his hand and I gave him mine. He squeezed it.

"Keep those mouse traps set!" He grinned and his little mustache wiggled.

"I will!"

71

He leaned toward me and I could smell his shaving lotion. Now was the time! He kissed my cheek. *Give him the tract!* My heart raced. *What if it makes him angry? What if he bawls me out? Give it to him!*

"So long, Mab."

"Mr. Wright!" I held on to his hand. "Here's something to read on the plane!" I forced the little square into his hand.

"Say! Thanks!" He jammed it into his pocket. He was gone.

What a coward I am! I don't have the right to sing, "Onward Christian Soldiers."

Father in heaven, please make Mr. Wright read the little message and save his soul. Forgive me for being so afraid.

"If anyone is ashamed of me and my words, the Son of Man will be ashamed of him when he comes in his glory and in the glory of the Father and of the holy angels" (Luke 9:26).

Rare Birds

"Is it okay with you if I invite Marlene and her husband for dinner next Saturday?" I asked my husband.

"Fine with me if you won't fuss. You have too much to do as it is."

"I won't fuss—too much." But I already had big plans. Marlene and Reggie were well-off and lived in a smart condominium in a nice part of the city. Everything would have to be super-super-duper.

"I'm not a very good cook," I told my neighbor one evening that week, "but I want to serve an exotic meal."

"Anyone can cook if she follows a recipe," she said. "Why not serve something you do well? How about your spaghetti and meatballs?"

I snorted. "That's not exotic! I want to serve something that will impress them!"

"We've still got pheasants in the freezer from Clyde's last hunting trip. I'll give you some."

"Pheasants! That's exotic! Thank you! I can borrow my mother's lace tablecloth. I'll really have to clean the house, too. I want everything to be perfect."

That Saturday I was pretty crabby to the family while I scrubbed, waxed, vacuumed and cooked.

"I've heard of the White Tornado," my husband growled, "but I live with the Black Thundercloud."

I followed the recipe for roast pheasant right down to the last pinch of marjoram, and baked it exactly two hours at 350 degrees. My good dishes looked fine on Mother's tablecloth and the house was as nice as I could make it.

When Marlene and Reggie rang the bell I opened the door in my one-and-only hostess gown and smiled in what I hoped was a gracious hostess manner.

"Darling," I said to my husband imperiously, "light the candles, please."

73

With pride I served the golden brown pheasants, green beans a la creole and Monarch combination salad. I sat with lowered eyelids, waiting for the compliments to begin.

Suddenly my husband choked. "Yuk! My bird needs a tourniquet!"

I looked up, horrified.

Reggie had a dismal look on his face. "Mine could use a Bandaid," he said apologetically.

Sure enough, bright red blood oozed out of the drumstick joints. Tears sprang to my eyes and I stood up. How could this have happened? I had followed the recipe exactly. This was to be the perfect dinner.

"Oh, please don't cry!" Marlene said. "It's not your fault. Probably your oven thermostat is out of adjustment."

In a blur of tears I whisked the bloody birds off and blotted the plates with a paper towel. I stomped to the refrigerator, got lunchmeat and peanut butter, and slapped them on the table.

We ate the fancy beans and salad in silence for awhile, then Reggie said, "I'll tell you a little secret. I *hate* pheasant. And I love peanut butter."

Marlene's eyes were almost shut with merriment as she held a napkin to her mouth. She was nodding her head up and down.

Pretty soon I began to grin, and then we all began to laugh.

I guess I'll have to re-cook those exotic birds. Or maybe there's a recipe that calls for half-baked, bloody pheasant.

You would think I'd know by now. Every time I try

to appear higher than I am, I always end up lower.

Lord Jesus, forgive me for pride. Forgive me for trying to appear more accomplished than I am.

"For everyone who exalts himself will be humbled, and he who humbles himself will be exalted" (Luke 14:11).

"A man's pride brings him low..." (Proverbs 29:23a).

Stars and Stripes— Forever?

"Isn't it wonderful to have this day at home?" I exclaimed to my husband at lunchtime.

"Sure is," he agreed. "A few hours to do as we please."

"But did you notice? Ours is the only flag on this whole block."

He stood up and sauntered over to the calendar.

"Oh, oh," he said with a worried look.

"What?"

"It's the Fourth of July."

"Oh, you character. Seriously, what's the matter with our neighbors?"

"Beats me. Maybe the Communists have done their job too well. People are so confused as to which day to put out the flag they would rather ignore the custom than be laughed at if they are wrong. Or maybe people have just quit caring."

"I'll bet George Washington and Paul Revere and all those other boys who fought so hard for our independence would kick themselves if they could see what we're doing with their freedom."

"It *is* a shame. I'll admit there is plenty wrong with our country but it's still the best place in the world to live."

I went to the window and looked at our flag. A gentle wind was making puffy ripples in it. A beautiful sight.

"Isn't there anything we can do?" I said.

"You and I ought to be willing to learn some facts about the people who run for office. I admit, I'm lax. I always feel I don't have enough time to read all the literature."

"Me too."

"But we should. And then we ought not only to vote, but see if anybody needs a ride."

"Encourage others."

"Yes. And even if we're alone we'll keep on hanging out Old Glory." He came and stood beside me. "And pray that God will keep on being merciful to us."

I pledge allegiance to the flag, and to the republic for which it stands. One nation, under God, indivisible, with liberty and justice for all.

Dear Father, most of the time I just pray for me and

mine and somehow don't have the faith to really pray for my nation. But I pray today. Please hold back the Communists. Oh God, please continue Thy watchful care and mercy over our United States of America.

"I urge, then, first of all, that requests, prayers, intercession and thanksgiving be made for everyone— for kings and all those in authority, that we may live peaceful and quiet lives in all godliness and holiness. This is good, and pleases God our Savior, who wants all men to be saved and to come to a knowledge of the truth" (I Timothy 2:1-4).

Square Shooter

After Sharon quit I didn't see much of Judy Smith, the girl whose boyfriend believed in reincarnation. She brought her lunch and I usually ate with either Alice or Marlene. However, I had studied a little about the Eastern religions and had a few scriptures ready to show her if I had the opportunity.

Yesterday morning the time came. We got to work at the same time and no one else was in the department. She came right to my desk.

"You were going to show me in the Bible why you don't believe in reincarnation."

"I know," I said. She sat down in Christy's chair as I reached for my Bible.

"Some good verses are in the first chapter of Philippians where Paul was writing to the Christians in Philippi. In verse 21 he wrote: 'For to me, to live is Christ and to die is gain.' Everything he did in his life was *for* Jesus and he believed when he died he was going to be *with* Him. If Paul thought he was going to become a mouse I don't think he would have called it gain, do you?"

Judy shook her head thoughtfully.

"And then in verses 23 and 24 he wrote: 'I am torn between the two: I desire to depart and be with Christ, which is better by far; but it is more necessary for you that I remain in the body.'

"He didn't say, 'I desire to depart and become a mouse.' He stated emphatically that when he died he would go to be with the Lord—zoom."

Judy's mouth opened, then she began to smile. "Let me see that."

I pointed to the words.

"Here's another good one," I said, turning the pages. "Second Corinthians 5:8: 'We are confident, I say, and would prefer to be away from the body and at home with the Lord.' Can you think of anyone you would rather be than yourself? I don't think Paul would have preferred to be away from his body to become another person—much less a mouse!"

Judy took the Bible and read it for herself.

"And Judy," I said, "if a person believes in reincarnation he can't believe in Jesus Christ as the Savior."

"Why not?"

"Didn't you tell me that the whole idea of reincarnation is to get all the imperfections worked out? So—if by taking on many lives we could eventually get rid of all the sin, Christ didn't need to die on the cross to pay for our sins."

She tapped her lips with a forefinger.

"I think you're right. I used to go to church when I was a kid."

"Did you ever accept Christ?"

"They used to ask you to come up front for some reason but I was always too bashful. But I believe in God."

She stood up suddenly and peered around at the clock.

"Want to see pictures of the house we're buying?"

"Sure," I said as I put King James back on the shelf. "You mean you and your folks?"

"No. My boyfriend and me." She handed me a picture envelope. "It's our first house and we're so thrilled." She looked at me with clear, honest eyes. She was a pretty girl, wholesome-looking and sweet.

She showed me several views of a brand new house.

"We're looking forward to doing our own landscaping. We can hardly wait to move in."

"When do you plan to get married?" I asked.

Her eyes lost their animated sparkle and became large and sad.

"I don't know. Sometime. Buck says we're so happy the way we are he doesn't want it spoiled."

"That leaves you in a shaky position, doesn't it? I mean, if you're going to help buy the house."

"Buck would never cheat me. He's a square shooter."

Judy, Judy, Judy! It seems to me Buck has already cheated you. I for one don't think he's a square shooter.

Dear Lord, I pray for Judy. You can see she wants to get married. Please change Buck's heart and straighten out their lives.

"The body is not meant for sexual immorality, but for the Lord, and the Lord for the body" (I Corinthians 6:13b).

"Marriage should be honored by all, and the marriage bed kept pure, for God will judge the adulterer and all the sexually immoral" (Hebrews 13:4).

Dispose-All?

It happened again today and my husband still isn't speaking to me. Isn't it reasonable to suppose that the garbage disposal is for the disposing of garbage? My husband seems to think it is primarily for grinding down water because he has given me a long list of Do Not Put Ins.

Since I've been working I seldom cook what he calls "good plain food" like chicken and noodles or vegetable beef stew, because those things take time. But today is Saturday and I decided to cook him a big old-fashioned beef stew with carrots, celery, potatoes, tomatoes and onions.

All of these things have peelings and it seemed logical to me to put them in the garbage disposal. I had a fleeting qualm after I had packed in the last scrap of celery strings because I sort of remembered they were on his list. However, I thought "garbage is garbage" and flipped on the switch. There was a click, then silence. I pushed the reset button. It still wouldn't work.

I felt terrible because nothing seems to upset my husband as much as a goofed-up garbage disposal. Last time he threatened to remove the whole unit if it got stopped up again. I think he is unfair because anyone could let an S.O.S. pad get in with the garbage, or accidentally drop a pop can tab in the sink.

Probably one reason he's such a fanatic on the subject is because one time he ripped his finger open on a nail I had dropped into the disposal when I was hanging little pictures around the sink.

"Why don't you put your hand down there and feel around before you turn it on?" he asked that day while he squeezed blood out of the wound.

"Ooh—it's so icky."

"But you don't mind if I put my hand in."

I thought of that this morning, so before I told him the dumb thing was messed up again I reached in and pulled all the peelings out of it, plus a slice of spoiled lunchmeat and two pieces of burned toast. I even tried to move the bottom part around with the pronged thing, but it was jammed.

"Guess what?" I said brightly to my husband out in the garage. He was cleaning parts for LTD and had grease up to his elbows.

"That crazy old garbage disposal is acting st-w-ange again."

He tensed up and knocked over the pan of gasoline and parts.

81

It didn't take him long to find the trouble in the disposal and now it's working beautifully again. I can't say as much for our relationship.

I don't know when he'll break his vow of silence. I may have to remind him that the Lord says not to let the sun go down upon his wrath.

And dear Lord, remind me never, never to put things in the garbage disposal that will stop it up. In other words, Lord, make me obedient to my husband.

"He who heeds discipline shows the way to life, but whoever ignores correction leads others astray" (Proverbs 10:17).

". . . and the wife must respect her husband" (Ephesians 5:33b).

Bible Teechur

This morning Jim Jorgensen came to my desk with a worried expression on his face.

"I have to go to a hearing this morning on behalf of the company, and I know it will drag on into the afternoon." He put some papers on my desk. "Can you meet with the people in the Bible study? I hate to cancel it because we're doing so well, especially now that we have those two men from Alice's department."

"But I can't teach!" I protested. My heart was already beating double time.

"Sure you can," he said gently. "Just read the seventh chapter of Romans, then lead a discussion."

"But—"

"If our Jesus could enable me to teach He can do the same for you." He started to walk away, then turned his big hulk around and grinned. "Remember Moses!" He laughed, but I didn't.

At lunchtime I couldn't swallow, not even yogurt. My insides felt like gelatin in an earthquake. My hands were sweaty. Besides our regulars—Mitzi, Marlene, Alice, Bea and me—there were the two drafters from Alice's department and another man I'd never seen.

We had quit using Jim's office awhile back and now met in one of the conference rooms. I sat down in Jim's place. Everyone looked at me expectantly.

"Jim had to be in court today," I explained. My upper lip felt as though there was a thread attached to it and someone above me jerked it from time to time. I couldn't control it. I put an index finger under my nose and pressed hard.

"We're supposed to read the seventh chapter of Romans," I said in a peculiar voice, "then discuss it." I looked around quickly. Everyone looked kind, interested. I felt a slight easing of tension.

"Would one of you gentlemen be kind enough to open in prayer?"

As though prearranged, the older draftsman leaned forward and prayed, "God in heaven, help us understand Your word. Be with Jim at the hearing and help this young lady as she teaches. In Christ's name, amen."

I took a deep breath. I was with my brothers and sisters in Christ. This was family. I relaxed.

I don't remember what I said or what they said. I only know I was happy and the hour seemed like five minutes.

On the way down to Personnel on the escalator, Bea Simpson, the lady who always has coffee and cigarettes for lunch, stood on the stair above me.

"Can we have lunch together one day this week?" She spoke in such a low voice I could barely hear her. I looked back at her. Her green eyes were pleading.

"Certainly! Tomorrow?"

"It's a date."

I have heard people talk about it, and I have even said I was there, but now I really know what it means to be on cloud nine.

Thank You, Lord, thank You for the wonderful experience of leading a Bible study. Thank You for taking over and doing it through me.

"On that day you will realize that I am in my Father, and you are in me, and I am in you" (John 14:20).

Hard as ABC

At retreat last year the speaker said something about our having mountaintop experiences to prepare us for the valleys of life below. I know now what he means. I was so happy at noon today. I thought I was smart for teaching the Bible class, but evidently I don't even know my ABC's.

Right after lunch Howard called, "Please get Joe Rudford's file for me."

I hurried into Records and found a file for Ralph Rudford, but no Joe Rudford.

When I told Howard I couldn't find it, he frowned. "Strange. I took it to Records myself yesterday."

Together we went back to the file room. Bea gave me a sympathetic wink. Howard opened the same drawer I had just looked in. I stood there with a smug look on my face.

"Here we are!" he said and plucked out the folder.

I followed him back to my desk, cheeks fiery red.

Then, just before closing time he asked, "You did send a letter and application to Norman Rogers?"

Norman Rogers, Norman Rogers? Did I? I looked through the alphabetical file we kept at my desk. Nope—no carbon copy to a Norman Rogers.

Howard had that familiar puzzled, weary look. "Hmm. I was certain I signed that letter."

He flipped through the file and in three seconds had the carbon in his hand.

Yes sir, I surely know what that speaker at retreat meant. I was so high at noon; now I'm in the pits.

I know my ABC's. And I know what my problem is. I am not thorough and I lack concentration. I want to be a good testimony to Howard. He probably thinks I'm so "heavenly minded I'm no earthly good."

Lord, I've done it again. Forgive me, please, for being proud of myself. I know I didn't teach the Bible class anyway. You did it. Please work through me to make me an efficient secretary. That's what I'm getting paid for.

"For by the grace given me I say to every one of you: Do not think of yourself more highly than you ought, but rather think of yourself with sober judgment, in accordance with the measure of faith God has given you" (Romans 12:3).

King's Kid

Bea and I had lunch in the cafeteria. For once I saw her eat something—a hard boiled egg and a tiny mound of cottage cheese. When she was young I am sure she could have won a beauty contest. She still had a lovely face but she was at least twenty-five pounds too heavy.

"I'm so fat," she said at lunch, "and I hate it. I diet okay during the day. The evenings are my downfall."

She didn't say anything else during lunch and I began to wonder why she wanted to be with me. She wiped her mouth on a napkin and said, "Mind if I smoke?"

"Go ahead." I smiled at her. "I used to smoke, too."

"You? How did you quit?"

I looked at my watch.

"I don't know if we have time. It's a long story."

"I'd like to quit; that's one of the things I wanted to talk about."

"Okay—I'll try to tell it fast. I had to go to the dentist—my mouth was really bothering me. And that wasn't the only thing. My husband and I were having too many parties, drinking too much and quarreling all the time. Our marriage was headed for trouble."

"Do I ever know what you mean," Bea said.

"The dentist told me *all* my teeth had to come out!"

"Oh, no."

"To be toothless seemed to me to be the end of the world. But I was in such pain I had to go through with it. And we didn't have the money. It seemed in that one hour my whole world crumbled.

"The day he started the extractions he put Novocaine in, then said we'd have to wait about fifteen minutes. I asked if I could smoke and he said 'yes,' then told me that he used to smoke and had quit. Like you, Bea, I wanted to know how he had done it."

"Well, for heaven's sake, tell me what he said."

"He had accepted Jesus Christ as Master and Lord of his life. He threw away his cigarettes and never smoked again."

"Wonderful! I wish I could do that," Bea said and put out her cigarette.

"You can! I did, although it was harder for me. The

87

Lord took away the desire to drink overnight but I
hung on to the cigarettes awhile. I knew I was a
Christian, that I had been saved as a free gift from
God and that my salvation didn't depend on what I
did. But one evening while I was holding the Bible in
one hand and a cigarette in the other, I knew I would
never be really happy until I quit."

"How did you actually do it?" Bea said, and lit
another cigarette.

"I think when I got it through my head that I
couldn't be really happy and continue to smoke, the
battle was almost won. Then I asked my best friend
and the pastor's wife to pray for me. And I asked my
husband to keep his cigarettes in the car. As soon as
he left for work I'd dump all the ashtrays and put
Christian literature in their place."

"Were you ever tempted to smoke again?"

"Lots of times. But every time I felt myself weak-
ening I prayed. One time I went to the bedroom,
flopped on my knees and practically yelled at the
Lord, 'You are the only reason I want to quit! Help
me!'

"He did. One of the weapons I used was reading.
You know how you want a cigarette after meals? I
kept articles and tracts, things I looked forward to
reading close by, so when I felt that urge I picked up
something about the Lord. By the time I'd read it, I
had forgotten the desire to smoke."

"How long has it been?"

"Years! And by His grace I'll never smoke again."

"Well," Bea said, "I certainly wish the Lord would
do that for me."

We sat in silence for a few minutes.

"Tell me," Bea continued, "do you think drinking

is a sin?"

"I found it a real problem."

"I think my husband and I are drinking too much. And we're also quarreling all the time."

"Alcoholics Anonymous says that if drinking is making a problem in your life, you may be addicted. Alcohol is a dangerous thing to fool around with." I drank my coffee and thought of those other, sad times. It seemed to be another person's life, my life without Christ.

"Will you pray for me?" Bea asked. Her stoic mask was gone and she seemed near tears.

"You know I will. Bea, have you ever accepted Christ?"

She nodded thoughtfully. "I think I did when I was little. I loved Sunday School and I loved Jesus."

"Well... why don't you make sure? Accept Him right now and you will be sure you're one of His children, with all the rights and privileges. I'll pray for you but you can pray for yourself. Just tell Him you've messed up—He knows it anyway—and that you need His help. Like Jim says, we're *King's* kids."

When I first met Bea a few months ago I never would have suspected she had a problem. She seemed so calm, efficient and in control.

Lord, thank You for the privilege of encouraging one of the family today. Help her mind to be in control of her body and not the other way around.

"Therefore, prepare your minds for action; be self-controlled; set your hope fully on the grace to be given you when Jesus Christ is revealed. As obedient children, do not conform to the evil desires you had when you lived in ignorance. But just as he who called you is holy, so be holy in all you do" (I Peter 1:13-15).

Hypocrite

One day Bobbie Simmons clicked by my desk and without stopping murmured, "Come to my office."

Obediently I jumped up and followed her.

"Shut the door," she commanded, but there was a merry twinkle in her eyes. When I closed the door, she grinned her wide, toothy smile. She really looked adorable when she had that expression on her face.

"Just heard a funny joke," she said and laughed.

The Holy Spirit poked me but I ignored Him. Bobbie proceeded to tell a hilariously funny, dirty joke. She told it with expressions and gestures; she told it well. I couldn't help but laugh.

"Thought you'd enjoy it," she said as I left her office.

Back at my desk all laughter stopped and I was miserable. Without a doubt I had to be the poorest testimony Christ had ever had. I didn't blame Bobbie for telling the joke but I was sick at heart for (1) being such a namby-pamby Christian in front of her that she thought I would enjoy the joke; and (2) for allowing her to tell it. What was the matter with me?

Why hadn't I at least said, "Hold on Bobbie, is it clean?"

I couldn't concentrate on my work. I felt I needed a bath. "I'm sorry, Lord," I kept praying but I felt like I was talking to a slab of granite. Finally I couldn't stand it. I went into Bobbie's office.

"May I see you a second?" I asked.

"Sure, babe. What can I do for you?"

I closed the door. My stomach felt as though I had had too much coffee and I could feel perspiration in my armpits.

"Bobbie, I want to apologize to you for being a hypocrite."

She grinned. "Is this a joke?"

"No, it's no joke. I stand around and quote scripture, go to the Bible class, even teach it sometimes, and act holy, then come in here and listen to a dirty joke. No wonder you don't have any faith in Christianity."

Her smile faded and she looked at me steadily. Her mouth got hard.

"I didn't think the joke was *that* bad," she said. "Sorry you got bent out of shape." She looked down at a stack of applications and picked up a pencil as though to dismiss me.

"Bobbie, I'm not blaming you for telling the joke. You've never pretended to be anything except what you are. You're honest. But I've made a profession to follow Christ. I don't have any business listening to off-color jokes."

She looked at me, her face non-committal. Then her cocky, sardonic smile returned.

"All right. I forgive you. But don't let it happen again!"

91

Apologizing to Bobbie was worse than going to the doctor for a shot. But I had to do it, and I'm glad it's over.

Lord Jesus, I know that the temptation to tell and listen to dirty jokes is my besetting sin. I am ashamed. I ask Your forgiveness. Please help me to overcome. I don't want to be a hypocrite.

"How can you say to your brother, 'Brother, let me take the speck out of your eye,' when you yourself fail to see the plank in your own eye? You hypocrite, first take the plank out of your eye, and then you will see clearly to remove the speck from your brother's eye" (Luke 6:42).

Boot Taboo

Maybe I will get a pair of boots. I've wanted a pair for a long time but they cost so much. Also, every year someone says they aren't in style anymore. But almost all the women at work have them. I almost bought a pair last month but didn't feel right about spending so much money. Instead I bought a pair of black sling pumps with crepe soles. When I look straight down they are quite dressy looking, but from the side they look like orthopedic tennis shoes. I didn't like them from the start but they *are* comfortable.

The first day I wore them to work, Bonnie, the model, said, "Oh, new shoes! Hey, they'd look great with pants!"

Why had I worn a dress?

As I walked around the office that day I soon learned rubber soles on carpeting make one stumble. After I had lurched into a couple of offices I learned to lift my feet up high, sort of like a cat on a wet floor. I was walking around in this pussy-foot manner when Judy jumped up to help me.

"Are you sick?" she asked.

"Oh, no," I assured her. "Just trying to keep from falling."

She bit her lip, shook her head and sat down.

By concentrating I managed to keep from stumbling the rest of the morning, but in mid-afternoon while Howard was interviewing I forgot all about my shoes. As I entered Howard's office with two cups of coffee I sang out, "Refreshments, gentlemen!"

I didn't quite spill coffee directly on the applicant, but only because he had split-second reactions. He leaped to his feet just as the coffee leaped out at him.

"Christy," I said later in the day, "payday I think I'll get a pair of boots."

"Better think again," she said and looked at her own brown leather ones with wooden soles and heels. "They're nice, but they sure make a person stumble a lot."

Should I buy boots? Maybe. If I can find some on sale, without crepe or wooden soles, and if the heels aren't too high.

Lord, You said not to think too much about what we wear. Help me choose the right things but not always be thinking of self.

"I also want women to dress modestly, with decency and propriety, not with braided hair or gold or pearls or expensive clothes, but with good deeds, appropriate for women who profess to worship God" (I Timothy 2:9).

Twiggie

What a week this has been! Monday is always a hard day because of new starts. Then, Tuesday morning just as I got the typewriter uncovered and my work laid out, the phone rang. It was Howard. He started to speak, then choked. Finally he sobbed, "My wife died!"

Stunned, I couldn't think of anything to say. My mind wanted to say something about the Lord but I knew Howard would turn me off. I just kept saying, "Oh no, oh no."

In a moment he was back in control and said I would have to take care of things, but if I needed to ask him questions he would be home most of the time.

As soon as I told Dick Gallagher why Howard wouldn't be in, people began to ask questions.

"What was wrong with her?"

"She had cancer."

"Was she sick long?"

"I don't think so. Howard didn't talk about his family."

"Was she in the hospital?"

"No, she died in her sleep."

"How is he taking it?"

"He sounded—sad. But he's a strong person."

"Where is the funeral?"

"How about flowers?"

"I don't know; I'll send around a bulletin."

Then the telephone began to ring. Howard had lots of friends in the company and I think they all called that morning. And I had so much to do!

I soon realized why Howard never seemed to be on top of his work—because the top always got one more application put on it! I had decided to work through lunch hour, even though it was Bible study day, when Jim called.

"My wife has had an accident," he said. "I'm going to have to rush home and take her to the doctor. I don't think it's too serious but I'll miss the lunch hour. Will you lead today?"

Oh no! Not today.

"Don't worry, Jim. Take good care of your wife."

Maybe it was the news about Howard's wife or Jim's wife—but all of us were extra close that day in Bible study. Recently two executive secretaries had joined the class, and although they were high on the ladder at work they were just our sisters in Christ.

The Bible study was an oasis of fellowship for me that day. I had a strange sensation—it seemed as though I was watching myself teach! I said several intelligent things that I didn't know I knew! The Lord had charge that day.

In fact He took charge the rest of the week. Somehow, between telephone calls to Howard and help from the other recruiters, the work went on—routing applications, making travel arrangements, interviewing, preparing offer letters. Mr. Gallagher complimented me on a smooth operation. (Thank You, Lord.)

But I was tremendously relieved when I saw Howard at his desk Friday morning. I brought him up-to-date on the work, then got him a cup of coffee. His face looked haggard, yet puffy. My heart went out to him. I started to walk away but the Lord wouldn't let me.

"Howard," I said, with my hands behind my back, "I'm so sorry about your wife. But the Lord never makes mistakes. My husband and I pray for you every night."

His eyes grew moist and he cleared his throat. He didn't look angry at all, just beaten.

"Thank you. Thank you very much. I appreciate your prayers."

Like the preacher said, there are no atheists in foxholes.

Lord Jesus, let this be the time I can talk to Howard about You. And thank You for getting me through the hardest week of my life.

"I am the vine; you are the branches. If a man remains in me and I in him, he will bear much fruit; apart from me you can do nothing" (John 15:5).

Stains in the Rain

Ever since Howard's wife died it seems we have been swamped with work. Yesterday I worked as fast and hard as I could all day, but at quarter to five my "in" box was still piled high. I didn't want to leave all that unfinished work in plain sight and have people think I wasn't doing my job, so I decided to hide it in my personal drawer, then come in early today and get caught up.

I took out my purse, put the Kleenex on top of my desk, moved the hand lotion and hairspray over to one side, then crammed in all the work. I felt a little deceitful, but the top of my desk looked great. I took some letters in for Howard to sign, and when I came back I sniffed the air.

"Christy, do you smell perfume? Or bubble gum?"

She sniffed the air. "I don't smell anything. Must be your imagination."

I shrugged, then took my cup into the ladies' room to wash it. When I returned Christy said, "Do you hear that hissing? Be quiet, now, and listen."

I cocked my head to one side. "I don't hear anything. It must be *your* imagination."

"No it isn't!" She put her hand up for quiet. "Sounds like escaping gas. But," she grinned impishly, "since there hasn't been an explosion—"

"Wait! I hear it!" I yanked open the desk drawer. There was the hissing noise. There was the perfume-bubble gum smell. Christy's eyes got even bigger as I picked up one dripping paper, then another, and another.

"What happened?" she whispered.

97

"Ar-rgh! When I put away my work I must have forced the head of the hairspray against the side. And it spewed out all over everything!"

Unfortunately most of those wet papers were applications. Fortunately it had been raining for three days, and I hoped Howard wouldn't ask me what happened but would blame the rains for the stains.

Ah, Holy Spirit—don't give up on me. When I do anything underhanded the Lord catches me. It wasn't wrong for me to put my work away—it was my motive.

Thank You Lord for not letting me get away with it. I know You are trying to perfect me.

"If you do what is right, will you not be accepted? But if you do not do what is right, sin is crouching at your door; it desires to have you, but you must master it" (Genesis 4:7).

Negative Exposure

"How do you like your job by now?" I asked Christy one day after she had been on board for about six weeks.

"It's okay. For now." She grinned wickedly. Christy had enrolled in some night classes at City College.

I had no doubt she would keep her word and go to the top.

"You don't really like your job, do you?" she asked.

"Yes I do!"

She made a sly face.

"No, I mean it. I'm grateful for such a good job in a super company."

"Grateful? You're kidding. You're qualified for a lot better job right here at Jenkins." She pointed to a list.

"Oh, I doubt that I—"

"Don't you ever read the Job Postings? There are two openings for Senior Secretaries this week. Then, it's just a step away to Administrative Aid, then—"

"I'm not that interested in a career. I'm just working to help my husband."

"And what if he should die?"

"Christy!"

"Well? Then you'd need a career, right?"

I didn't answer.

"So if you're going to work, why not have the best?" she finished with a triumphant look in her eyes.

She was right. If I could earn more money for the same hours and stay in this company, why not? That afternoon I went to the main lobby and studied the Job Posting Board. I felt I could qualify for one of the Senior Secretary positions. After I had filled out the forms I showed them to Christy.

"The only hitch is," I said, "I have to get Howard to sign it."

"So?"

"So, he's been nice to me. It might hurt his feelings.''

She looked amused.

"You're too tenderhearted. Think only of yourself. He'll get another secretary."

I took the papers in to Howard and he accepted the idea as standard procedure.

"I would hate to lose you but I would never stand in your way of advancement," he said as he signed his name.

I submitted the application and was interviewed. I waited. I thought about it all the time. It would be over a hundred a month increase and better working conditions.

"Don't count on it," my husband advised.

"Don't be negative!" I said.

"Anyway, I want you to quit as soon as we get straightened out," he added.

After three weeks I was turned down.

"I didn't want the dumb job anyhow," I told myself, but a seed of discontent was sown. Instead of looking forward to my job each morning I found fault. It didn't help for Christy to point out other positions on the Job Posting Board.

"Christy!" I exploded one day, "I'm not going to try again! You got my hopes up once and I felt terrible when they turned me down. I'm not going through that again."

"You'll never get promoted with that attitude," she taunted. "You're negative!"

"Negative! I'm not negative."

I was hurt and angry. "Maybe it's not God's will for me to change jobs," I said piously.

"But what if it is? Where's your faith?"

I was so surprised my mouth dropped open. Christy talking to *me* about faith?

"Christy! What *do* you believe?"

"I'se a Baptist." Her usual, flawless diction sounded like a Civil War slave.

"Are you kidding me?"

"No, ma'am. Ah believed when Ah wuz a chile. Now my daddy's tryin' to make a Jehovah's Witness out of me."

I didn't know whether or not to believe her. Sometimes I felt close to her but other times I felt mixed-up. She could make me feel good and make me feel stupid. I wanted to be a good testimony before her but it seemed I was always losing my temper or saying something off-color.

Now she tells me she believes, I thought. *Does she?* I had been so self-centered recently I had forgotten all about the Lord putting Christy beside me for a purpose. Maybe I *had* been negative. What would be the best example to her—to try for a better job or to be content with what I had?

"One thing's sure, Christy, we'll both lose *these* jobs if we don't quit talking."

Negative? Huh. I always thought I was a ray of sunshine. Why trust when you can worry?

Dear Lord, I admit I feel negative. Ever since I first applied for that other job I've been edgy, worried and covetous. I would really like to earn more money and have prestige, and all—forgive me. Help me to count my blessings.

"Do not love the world or anything in the world. If anyone loves the world, the love of the Father is not in him. For everything in the world—the cravings of sinful man, the lust of his eyes and the boasting of what he has and does—comes not from the Father but from the world. The world and its desires pass away, but the man who does the will of God lives forever" (I John 2:15-17).

"Do not be anxious about anything, but in everything, by prayer and petition, with thanksgiving, present your requests to God" (Philippians 4:6).

No Problem

"Why are we buying all this fruit?" my husband asked when he looked into the shopping cart. "Peaches, cantaloupe, bananas, oranges. A whole pineapple?"

"You know the custom in Personnel to bring goodies on birthdays?"

"I know. Groceries are costing me more, but I'm eating less."

"It's Howard's birthday tomorrow."

"You're giving him a pineapple?"

"He's on a sugar-free diet. He never gets to eat any of the goodies."

"Neither do I."

"So I thought I would bring a platter of fresh fruit."

"How can you manage all that juicy stuff?" He sampled a grape.

"I'll have to get up a little early to peel the fruit but I'll arrange it there. No problem."

By concentrating the next morning I remembered to take the big platter, plastic forks, paper plates, and decorations, besides the prepared fruit in plastic containers.

Although it had taken forty-five minutes to prepare the fruit, I was still the first one in the office. I rushed into Howard's room, took out the platter and carefully arranged the fruit: banana chunks in the center, a ring of stewed prunes, peach and apple slices, then orange sections, cubed watermelon and cantaloupe, half pineapple slices, and the whole platter garnished with maraschino cherries. I put the arrangement right in the center of Howard's desk. It was beautiful!

Then I began to decorate his office. I took out the "Happy Birthday" sign I had painted the night before and taped it on the wall behind his chair, then draped twisted crepe paper streamers from the sign to both sides of the room. I had put all the sticky containers back into the sack and had started to step out of the office to admire the whole scene when I saw a big, dark stain on the desk blotter. What on earth? I stepped closer.

The stain was about two inches wide all around the platter and growing. I touched it. It was drippy and sticky. Fruit juice was oozing off the platter in a steady stream.

"Oh no!" I moaned.

Like a machine I plopped all the fruit back into the containers, poured the juice into the wastebasket, yanked off the sticky blotter, ran to the restroom for paper towels, ran to the supply room for a new blotter, rearranged the slightly dehydrated fruit, switched Howard's wastebasket for mine, put the containers back into the sack, ran to the restroom, rinsed my hands and fluffed out my hair, rushed back and uncovered my typewriter. I was sitting calmly at my desk when fellow employees began to bring Howard their goodies.

"Fresh fruit!" everyone exclaimed. "How could you do it!"

After everyone had left the office and Howard and I were alone he said, "This is the most thoughtful thing anyone has ever done for me."

He stuffed a piece of cantaloupe into his mouth. "Delicious! How did you manage all this? It must have been awfully hard!"

I beamed at him. "Really, Howard, it was no problem." (". . . that couldn't be solved," I said under my breath.)

All's well that ends well—but if I ever take fruit again, it will be arranged in a wash basin, not a platter.

Thank You Lord Jesus for giving Howard a nice day, for making everything turn out all right.

"And we know that in all things God works for the

good of those who love him, who have been called according to his purpose" (Romans 8:28).

Mending Ms.

Frankly I don't know why Bobbie Simmons thinks women's lib is so great. I guess I am a liberated woman but I can't see that it has done that much for me. I should have the same rights and privileges as my husband, right? Let us consider mending, for example. I cannot imagine giving him a pair of my slacks with an off-hand comment, "Oh babe—there's a little rip in these. Fix 'em when you get time, okay?" Or, "Honey, these panty hose have a tiny hole in the toe. Maybe you should mend it before it starts a run."

Are you *kidding?*

No. It's like cooking, washing and cleaning. Mending, even for working wives, still falls into our hands.

I despise mending. As soon as I approach the sewing machine I get tense. In the first place it is hardly ever threaded with the right color, so the first hurdle is to find a bobbin with the right thread—which of course is out of the question. I can't even find large things, like scissors and attachments in my sewing box. Consequently, most of my mending is white on black, or brown on pink or some other strange combination.

Probably the real reason I hate to mend is because I've never mastered the sewing machine. Sometimes

I think there's a demon lurking in the electric motor who delights in watching me think I am sewing up a seam while he's holding the bobbin thread in his hand. Another trick of his is to wad up one or two yards of thread and stuff them inside the bobbin case, which usually results in a broken needle.

Machine mending is bad enough but I'm even worse with a needle and thread. I avoid sewing on buttons until my husband has sadly twiddled a button thread in my sight two or three times. Even then sometimes I hand him a safety pin—if I can find one. I can usually find one in my slip straps because I hate to sew them back on, too.

Mending, in its pure form, is such a disagreeable thing to me that I have learned a lot of ways to avoid it—at least for awhile. For example, a hem can be glued in. But you should be careful to use waterproof glue; otherwise, it will wash out and you'll have to glue it in again. I have used staples for hemming, but they show because they catch the light. They also catch your hose.

Pants pockets can be mended real well with masking tape and will hold up for several washings if you don't use hot water. If you have two pair of panty hose with one bad leg each, cut off the bad legs and wear both pair. Marvelous tummy control.

I have never figured out an easy way to mend a ripped seam, so when I see one of those I either stuff the garment back in the dirty clothes hamper or get out the sewing machine. That's probably why my clothes hamper is full, even after washday. It's full of things no one is going to mend but *me.*

That's why I don't think women's lib is all that great. Surely it has opened up many new avenues of work for us. I can be a crane operator if I want to be. But until they can get a law passed that says husbands have to spend equal time mending, I think they've got a long way to go—Bobbie.

Mother says she used to have a rigid schedule: Monday, wash; Tuesday, iron; Wednesday, mend; Thursday, clean; Friday, bake; Saturday, market and cook; Sunday, church and rest. Hmm. Maybe I am sort of liberated.

Dear Lord, I know that mending is part of my job. Help me to work it into my schedule and not complain about it.

"A wife of noble character who can find? . . . out of her earnings she plants a vineyard . . . She sets about her work vigorously; When it snows, she has no fear for her household; for all of them are clothed in scarlet. . . . She watches over the affairs of her household . . ." (Proverbs 31:10a,16b,17a,21,27a).

Rise and Fall

"Take a look at that!" I proudly dropped a printed form in front of my husband's newspaper last night.

"Travel Authorization Worksheet," he read aloud. "What is it?"

107

"It's a form our whole department is going to use! Isn't it great?"

"Ta da! So what?"

"*I* made it! *I* designed it!"

He looked at it again.

"*Name, address, phone,*" he read aloud, "*interview with, position, leave, arrive, leave arrive, time, flight number, airline*—hey! You really figured all this out?"

I nodded, smiling, pleased as a little girl with her first mud pie.

"We all have to make travel arrangements for applicants who come for interview from some other city or state. Usually we have to call the person and ask if he is still interested in working at Jenkins and if he wants to come for an interview. If he does, we have to get a date from whoever is going to do the interviewing. Next we call the airline, reserve a flight, then call the applicant again with all the information."

My husband looked dazed. I didn't blame him. I had never made an appointment yet that I hadn't forgotten some of the details.

"It's really hard to remember everything. That's why I thought of this form. I made it up for Howard and me and Xeroxed a few copies. He showed it to Mr. Gallagher and *he* ordered it printed!"

"Well congratulations, baby," my husband said and kissed me. "I knew you were good for something!"

I picked up the copy and smiled at it. It looked so beautiful in printed form.

"I'm going to paste this copy in my diary," I said proudly. "With these forms I'll never again forget any details."

Then, like the pain of a stomach cramp, it hit me.

"Mr. Zabrinski!" I whispered.

"What?"

"Mr. Zabrinski! He's an applicant who is due in tomorrow, but he can't be!"

"He's sick?"

"No! Piping Section called this afternoon and said the supervisor was called to a job site. There's no one qualified to interview Mr. Zabrinski!"

"Did you call him?"

"No! That's it! I was so excited when Print Shop brought these in I forgot all about him! Oh," I wailed, close to tears, "the airline tickets cost $350! He'll be in Personnel at 8:00 in the morning!"

Brain, why do you fade in and out like a far-away radio station? Can't I ever depend on you?

Dear Lord, I beg You to help me out of this jam. It's all because of my ego. I know it's smart to be inventive on the job but to be dependable is so much better.

"Pride goes before destruction, a haughty spirit before a fall" (Proverbs 16:18).

The Whole Truth

We didn't sleep well last night. I worried about Mr.

Zabrinski and my husband worried about me. This morning I called Alice and told her I had to go in early. I wanted to be the first one to talk to Mr. Z. I had just arrived when he appeared in the waiting room. He was dark with doe-like brown eyes. His mustache curled on the ends and he wore a light tan and brown checked suit that was a half-size too big. He didn't look very important but I knew from his application he was a giant in piping design. The company wouldn't want him to quit before he was hired.

What could I say? I thought about telling him I had tried to call him but I couldn't do it. Even if I got fired I would have to tell him what happened. With a knot in my stomach I went to the waiting room. I stepped forward briskly, smiled and stuck out my hand as I had seen Bobbie do so many times.

"Mr. Zabrinski? I'm Howard Larson's secretary."

He smiled and shook my hand.

"So pleased to make your acquaintance," he said. He bowed so low I thought he was going to kiss my hand.

"Mr. Zabrinski, I've done an incredibly stupid and inconsiderate thing."

He quit smiling. "Oh? Yes?"

"Oh yes. The man who was to interview you today, a Mr. Cooper? He had an emergency out in the field. He had to leave town yesterday."

He rubbed his chin and frowned. "That is too bad."

"I could have called you but to be honest, I forgot."

There was silence. At last he spoke. "When do you think Mr. Cooper can see me?"

I smiled hopefully.

"He has you tentatively set up for a week from to-

110

day." I bit my lip. "I was supposed to cancel the flight and rearrange everything with you yesterday afternoon. I'm so sorry."

He took both my hands. He smiled gently.

"Don't worry. My brother lives here so already I took week's holiday. I visit with him first, then be interviewed." He gave my hands a squeeze. "It's okay!"

I couldn't believe this fantastic answer to prayer. I was off the hook.

Later in the day Howard called out from his office, "Did you talk to Mr. Zabrinski?"

"Sure did!" I called back. "Everything's okay for a week from today."

"Those forms you designed are already helping, aren't they?"

I was silent. I knew in my heart I would have to tell Howard the whole truth. But I could pick the time, couldn't I?

I probably won't sleep well again tonight. Talk about the pressures of business. About half my pressures are caused by *me*.

First Lord, thank You for having Mr. Zabrinski take a week's vacation. Now, Father, give me the courage to tell Howard the whole truth.

"The heart is deceitful above all things and beyond cure. Who can understand it?" (Jeremiah 17:9).

Hot Stuff

This morning Grant Hoffman, the recruiter who hires clerical personnel, started to go into Howard's office.

"He's interviewing, Grant," I said.

"Oh." He came to my desk and there was a naughty look in his deep-set eyes. His mustache twitched a little as he tried to keep from smiling.

"When he's through tell Howard there's something in the reception room that needs his immediate attention."

I nodded and scribbled a note.

Grant went into John Burgemeir's office, came out smiling, and in a second John came out with a bright look on his face and hurried into the reception room. Grant went on his way to all the recruiters' offices. One by one they went to the reception room.

When Howard's interview ended I hurried to his office with the note.

"Grant says there's something that needs your immediate attention in the reception room," I said.

Howard's eyes became glittery and there was a smirk on his lips.

"Everybody is going out there," I said. "What's it all about?"

"Why don't you go see?" he suggested.

I got there just as Don Braddock and John Burgemeir were coming back. Both men looked idiotic. Don rolled his eyes toward the ceiling. "Ooh la la!" he chortled.

"Wonder what skills she has?" John asked.

"Who cares!" Don moaned wickedly. "Wonder if

112

she'll work the night shift?" Both men broke into loud laughter.

I looked into the reception room and understood. She was probably somewhere between thirty and thirty-five. God had given her basic good looks and a beautiful figure, but she looked more like an applicant for a Las Vegas show than for an office.

Bright blue eye shadow and heavy false eyelashes made her eyes appear too big, and her rouge was the shape and color of a brick. Her lips were greasy red, and her hair fell in loose, brassy waves over her bare shoulders.

Her sundress was tight and cut low at the bust, revealing a generous cleavage. Although the skirt was full she had crossed her legs so that a good part of her thigh was exposed. On her feet were bright red, four-inch heel, baby-doll shoes.

As the girl worked on her application, Mitzi looked up at me and shook her head in disgust. As I stood there three more fellows filed in, wolfed in the sight and went back, shaking their fingers, rolling their eyes, smacking their lips.

It was disgusting. But I laughed too.

I wonder how that woman would feel if she knew that instead of the admiration she desperately wanted, her cheap appearance was not only ridiculed but caused several men to sin?

Dear Lord, help me to be modestly dressed at all times. I am sorry we are all such sinners. What a price You paid for our exceeding sinfulness.

"Then out came a woman to meet him, dressed like a prostitute. . . . Many are the victims she has brought down . . ." (Proverbs 7:10,26).

Jesus said, "But I tell you that anyone who looks at a woman lustfully has already committed adultery with her in his heart" (Matthew 5:28).

Stiff Neck

For five days in a row my neck has hurt. I thought maybe it was conviction for not telling Howard about Mr. Zabrinski, so I finally told him everything. He took it real well and only gave me a short lecture about how serious it could have been. I felt much better after I had told him but I still had a stiff neck.

"It's your job," Christy said. "You're too tense."

"It's your bed," Marlene advised. "Too soft."

"It's that flu," Alice said. "Better see a doctor."

"Your spine is out of line," my sister-in-law said. "Try my chiropractor; he won't hurt you although you might hear your bones crack!"

"Oh-h-h!" I moaned and trembled, but my neck hurt so badly I finally made an appointment. I was really trembling when I went into the dressing room.

The doctor didn't smile or make small talk. He made me face the wall in the paper gown, and after he had sized me up he said my body was out of line.

"It's like your wheels are out of balance. No

wonder you're in pain." Then he led me to a brown leather log, and before I could protest I was in a prone position.

"Now, pull your left knee up and keep your other leg straight," he commanded. He placed my hands in the same position as a corpse in a coffin.

"Take a deep breath," he barked. *(Father, is it my last?)* I tried to get up but he placed his knee on my leg so I couldn't get away, then pulled my shoulder with all his might. Bones cracked like the Fourth of July and my back felt like Labor Day.

"Splendid!" he said. "Now roll on your tummy, please."

He backed away about ten steps, scraped his feet like an angry bull and charged. That was the first time I had done a back bend since I was fifteen.

Then almost repentantly he stroked my neck. When I had almost forgiven him he grabbed my head by the ears and cracked it first to the left, then to the right. I was certain he had broken my neck. I was in shock the rest of the evening.

This morning when I awoke I sat up carefully. I eased my feet over the side, then stood up. I turned my head back and forth cautiously.

Then I yelled, "My stiff neck is gone!"

Whatever caused it I hope I don't have another stiff neck.

Dear Lord, I still think conviction caused part of my neck trouble. Help me live a transparent life, Lord Jesus, with no hidden uglies anywhere.

115

"Do not be stiff-necked ... submit to the Lord. ... Serve the Lord ..." (II Chronicles 30:8).

"You stiff-necked people, ... You always resist the Holy Spirit!" (Acts 7:51).

Bye, You All

"Pss-s-t!"

I looked over at Christy. She beckoned for me to scoot over close. Whenever she wanted to tell me anything I always had to go to her. Sometimes I rebelled at this tiny display of authority over me, but I always gave in. I scooted up close to her.

"Want to hear a secret?" she whispered, her eyelids half-closed.

"Sure." I bent my head over my steno pad as though studying the outlines. (Bad, the Holy Spirit prompted. You are not only a gossip, but deceitful.)

"Bobbie Simmons is being promoted," Christy whispered, her eyes excited. "She's transferring to New Orleans."

"Oh no!"

"Oh no? Aren't you glad for her? She's going up. She'll be in charge of that office."

"Of course. I am glad for her but I hate for her to go. It will be dead around here."

"Her secretary is going too."

"Louise is leaving? When are they going?"

116

"Two weeks. Everyone will know this afternoon. Mum 'til then." She put a slender finger on her mouth.

That afternoon Bobbie swaggered around the office. With her hands on her hips, or patting her hair, or touching her forehead with the back of her hand she gestured dramatically.

"Dahlin' I jest hate to leave you-all, but duty calls! Ah'm gonna have to go on dayown to New Orleeens and set those folks straight."

Bobbie was going to be missed!

Bobbie still wasn't saved.

On her last day I went into her office.

"Don't say goodbye!" she said quickly. "I'll be back!" She smiled a wide, phony smile. "Anyway, you're coming to my farewell party aren't you?"

I shook my head. "No. I'd rather remember you sober!"

"You mean you-all would begrudge little ol' me a little ol' mint julep?"

"Bobbie, I'm going to miss you."

"I'm going to miss you, too."

"Bobbie, if you're ever in danger—or *anything*— don't forget that Jesus loves you!"

The twinkle in her eye vanished and she looked at me steadily, honestly.

"I'll remember."

I turned to leave and she stood up.

"Hey!" she said softly. She gave me a quick hug. "You're pretty real—for a religious person."

It's not going to be the same without Bobbie. What a bright spot she has been.

Oh Lord! Please save Bobbie. What a brilliant light she could be for You. I'm sorry my light didn't shine brighter for her.

"No one lights a lamp and hides it in a jar or puts it under a bed. Instead, he puts it on a stand, so that those who come in can see the light" (Luke 8:16).

Cucumber Crisis

People who don't have to buy groceries on Saturday don't know what we go through. Only we Saturday shoppers who have to shove a loaded basket which is determined to go to the right when we go to the left can understand the problems and downright dangers that lurk in a crowded supermarket. Every forage is fraught with frustration and fear. What casual weekday shopper has ever been rammed full speed from behind by another frantic shopper trying to get her buying done before the morning is over?

Potential danger is everywhere—tumbling pyramids of cereal, kids on roller skates, Girl Scout cookies and puppies for sale. Saturday shopping is hard.

This morning I noticed one of my peers in terrible trouble. She had selected a cucumber from high on a sloped vegetable tray and the movement had started an avalanche. When I first saw her she was leaning forward, pushing at the bottom of the display with her stomach, arms outstretched over the shiny green ovals, legs spread-eagled. All she needed was a policeman to frisk her.

I ran forward to help and the moment I touched the cucumbers I was shocked and repelled.

"Slimy!" I cried. "What's on them?"

"Wax, I think—or grease." She moaned and pushed harder with her stomach.

"Why?" I yelled, trying to get a grip on the slithering things.

"Don't know," she whimpered. "Maybe—to keep—bugs off." She seemed to be getting faint. I tried harder to stop their downward progression by pushing with my stomach and arms too, but the more we tried the more of the slimy things dropped to the floor. They seemed to be alive, determined to get away.

"What are we going to do?" I panted. "I can't stay here all morning. I have a washing to do."

Others who either didn't realize what we were doing or didn't want to get involved pushed their baskets on by.

When my arms were getting numb the vegetable man came swinging through double doors from the back. His black eyes twinkled.

"Ah so! You leddies look velly funny. What you do?"

"Help!" we moaned in unison.

He soon had the greasy green giants whipped into position. Exhausted, we two who had stood in the gap went separate ways. Bless her heart. I should have gotten her name and phone number. We could have started a Cucumber Club, or maybe collaborated on a book. We could have called it, *The*

Catastrophic Consequences of Choosing a Cucumber.

Maybe I exaggerate a teensy bit, but no matter how you look at it it's not easy to be a career woman and a cottage keeper at the same time. There's so much to do!

Lord Jesus, only through You can I get everything done. Please help me weed out the nonessentials, make the time stretch, and increase my strength.

"Even youths grow tired and weary, and young men stumble and fall; but those who hope in the Lord will renew their strength. They will soar on wings like eagles; they will run and not grow weary, they will walk and not be faint" (Isaiah 40:30,31).

Green-Eyed Monster

"How was your day?" Alice asked as we started across the gigantic parking lot to her car.

"Fine. A little tiring because I've been teaching a new girl most of the day."

"Not to replace you?"

"Oh, no. She was hired to take Louise's place— you know, Bobbie's secretary. Right now the new girl doesn't have a boss because the man they hired to take Bobbie's place doesn't come on board until next Monday."

Alice unlocked her door and while I waited for her to reach over and unlock mine I noticed how bare the tree branches had become. It was darker now at five o'clock, and it felt like fall.

"She's so cute," I continued after I got in. "Her name is Cindy. Cindy Gaylord. She's about five foot three and skinny! Not scrawny-skinny but sexy-skinny, you know?"

Alice nodded and stared straight ahead, waiting her turn to leave the aisle we were in and get into the main stream of traffic headed for the freeway.

"But Cindy doesn't act sexy. She has a darling baby face, long blond hair—fixes it like Farrah Fawcett—and she's so funny! But gentle too. You'll have to come down and meet her."

Alice saw an opening and shot out into the street.

"Sounds like you like her," she said and glanced at me. "Did you invite her to Bible class?"

"I did," I answered. "But wouldn't you know? Christy had already invited her to lunch tomorrow. In fact, they had lunch together today."

"Christy. Is she the black girl beside you?"

"Yeah. From the moment Marlene brought Cindy around, Christy seemed to like her. I've never seen her show such an interest in anyone before." We were on the freeway now, headed home and I should have been happy and content, but I felt frustrated.

"I can't get over it," I groused. "When Christy is talking to Cindy she drops her intellectual facade and seems as friendly as a puppy. And Cindy talks to her as though they've known each other for ages."

121

"Sounds like you're jealous!"

"I think I am." *And hurt,* I added to myself. I started to tell Alice how Christy had *whispered* something in Cindy's ear and then both of them had laughed ... but it sounded so petty.

I looked out at five lanes of evening traffic. Thousands of cars, all rolling along together, yet inside each car was an individual little world which might be happy or sad or lonely. Tonight I felt like one of the cars. At Jenkins Company I was one of thousands of employees all traveling along together, but locked inside each person was an individual world. Christy and Cindy were in different cars and they had excluded me. I was sure it was because of Christianity. Maybe I had come on too strong for Christ. Whatever the reason, their shut-out hurt.

What's the matter with me? Why do I care? I have plenty of friends at church, and the people in the Bible class like me. What do I care about Cindy and Christy?

But Lord, You know I do care. I feel jealous and hurt. I know it's wrong, and that hurts. Help me. Comfort me.

"Blessed are you when people insult you, persecute you and falsely say all kinds of evil against you because of me. Rejoice and be glad, because great is your reward in heaven, for in the same way they persecuted the prophets who were before you" (Matthew 5:11,12).

Can A Leopard Change Its Spots?

Saturday I did it again.

Two years ago I did it and I promised my husband and my mother I would never do it again. And I most certainly promised myself if I ever did it again it would be done by a professional.

I don't know what happened Saturday. Maybe it was because my husband had to work and I was home by myself. Maybe it was because I found a grey hair or because Cindy had such beautiful blond hair—whatever—I succumbed to temptation.

It was as though some strange force caused me to skid to a stop in front of the drugstore, leap out of the car and rush to the cosmetic section. Within five minutes I had grabbed a kit, pushed through the check-out line and was back in the car.

Locked in the bathroom I clawed open the box and yanked out the directions. I scanned them quickly.

"I know all this," I mumbled impatiently. "Only this time I'll leave it on long enough. No more orange streaks if I have to leave it on two hours."

Painfully, I pulled tiny strands of hair through the holes in the dopey-looking bonnet. I thought ahead to the finished work. Would I look just a teensy bit like Farrah? Or Cindy? I began to hum, "There she goes, Miss America . . ."

Every few minutes I checked the color—not light enough, still too orange. Finally, after two full hours, the strands looked right—a lovely pale, pale blond. Carefully I removed the cap and looked into the mir-

123

ror. My heart dropped to sea level, closely followed by my stomach. True, the streaks were the right shade but some of the goop had seeped through the holes and had made orange spots all over my head. I looked like a leopard with the mange.

I *felt* like a leopard with the mange.

When my husband came home from work he almost got a hernia from laughing so hard.

"The preacher knew what he was talking about when he made me promise for better or for worse!" He howled and fell over in his chair, clutching his stomach.

I wore an old brown wig to church Sunday and we stopped at the drugstore on the way home and got some brown dye.

Today my hair doesn't look too bad if I stay out of the sunlight. And I've learned a lesson. I will never, never frost my hair again . . . unless of course, some new product comes on the market that guarantees it to be foolproof!

I've always said I would grow old gracefully. I think I lied.

Dear Lord, again I ask You to help me get my mind off myself. Make me thankful for the way You created me instead of always wishing I looked like someone else.

"So God created man in his own image, in the image of God he created him . . ." (Genesis 1:27).

"Shall what is formed say to him who formed it, 'Why did you make me like this?' " (Romans 9:20b).

Comforter

After Cindy had been on board about three weeks, I found her early one morning seated at her desk with her head on her arms. When I spoke her name she looked up, startled.

"Hi," she said, but there was no enthusiasm in her voice, and her nose and eyes were red.

Cindy hadn't told me much about her private life. All I knew was that she had wanted to get away from her folks who lived "up north" and that she lived in an apartment. Maybe she was crying because she was homesick. Whatever the reason, I felt sorry for her, even if she did like Christy better than me!

At my desk I took down King James and flipped through it; I hoped to find a verse of comfort I had underscored in the past. I put a piece of scratch paper in the typewriter and copied:

"God is our refuge and strength, a very present help in trouble" (Psalm 46:1).

I drew a happy face and signed the note, "Love, Mab." On the way to the restroom I tossed it on her desk.

When I got back, there was a folded piece of paper in the center of my desk with flowers drawn on it. Inside it read:

"Dear Mab, thank you so much for your concern. I

125

needed that! Could we talk sometime?" There were more flowers and her signature.

The next morning Cindy was waiting for me.

"Hope you're ready for me to cry on your shoulder," she said with a twisted little smile. We went into one of the empty offices and closed the door.

"Go ahead and cry," I said, trying to sound cheerful.

"Remember when you asked me to go to the Bible study?" she began. "I wanted to tell you then that I thought it was nice of you to invite me but I didn't think reading the Bible would help me—or maybe I wouldn't be allowed in the class."

She laughed softly and tried to put on a throaty tone—"Scarlet woman, not fit for decent people." She winked and tried to look wicked.

"Cindy, what are you talking about?"

"Okay. Are you ready?" She took a deep breath and let it out. "I've been living with a guy for over a year. I was brought up a strict Catholic. So you know what that means. Washed out."

"But you can always confess your sins, can't you?"

"You're supposed to confess and repent. I'm not sorry! I'm not even sure if it's sin anymore. Things are different. And it's not as though I was sleeping around. I really love him. And he loved me—even if he didn't want to get married. Now it's over."

Her baby face contorted as she tried not to cry. Instinctively I hugged her.

"It's not that I blame *him*," she said. "That was his point in not getting married. He said it might not work out, and he was right." She blew her nose softly. "It's just that the apartment is so lonely!" Her shoulders shook with her sobs.

What could I say? Tell her she's a sinner? *Now look here, Cindy,* I could hear myself say, *the Bible says you have sinned.* She wouldn't care about that. She wanted her man back. Lord, what can I say?

It seemed as though the Lord said, "Mab, be quiet. Love her. Don't condemn; I'll handle that. And remember, except for My grace you could be in the same position."

She quit crying and blotted her eyes and nose with a tissue.

"So now, Mabber, you know my deep, dark secret. I are a fallen woman."

I shrugged.

"Nobody is perfect, Cindy." We started out the door. "Just remember one thing: Jesus really *loves* you, no matter what."

Cindy—and Judy. Is this the kind of life you would want for your daughters?

Dear Father, help me be a comfort and a friend to Cindy. Above all, make a way for me to show her Your wonderful self. Then she will really be comforted.

"Praise be to the God and Father of our Lord Jesus Christ, the Father of compassion and the God of all comfort, who comforts us in all our troubles, so that we can comfort those in any trouble with the comfort we ourselves have received from God" (II Corinthians 1:3,4).

Key-Nut Squeaker

"Mab? This is Marlene. Forgive me for calling you at home so early but since it's John's birthday and Christy's on vacation, I knew you and I had better be sure to bring goodies today!"

"I remembered. In fact I've already put cupcakes in the trunk and cut some beautiful roses."

"Oh good. I was afraid you'd forget. Okay—see you at work."

"Alice? This is Mab. Hey, I'm sorry to tell you this, but I can't get the car started."

"Really? What's wrong?"

"I hate to tell you. I've lost the keys. You'd better go on without me."

"Marlene? Whew, I'm glad you're still at home. Uh, something unexpected came up and I'm going to be just a little late. Will you tell Howard when he gets in?"

"Oh? Sure. Don't worry."

"And please tell John I haven't forgotten him. I'll be there as soon as I can."

"Honey?"

"Mab? Where are you?"

"I'm home. Would it be possible for you to come home for a minute?"

"For a minute?" It's eighteen miles. What's wrong?"

"You're going to be so irritated with me."

"I know, but tell me."

"I can't find my keys."

"Not again. Did you look in the refrigerator?"

"Yes—I've looked everywhere. They're gone!"

"Okay, now that I'm home pour me some coffee and let's retrace your steps this morning."

"I got ready for work. I went out into the yard and cut roses for John Burgemeir's birthday. I put them and the cupcakes in the trunk—"

"Hold it. That's where they are."

"I wouldn't do a dumb thing like that!"

"See that little leather thing peeking out from under those wilted roses? There are some shiny brass things attached to it. Those are keys. What's the matter, baby—cat got your tongue?"

"Happy birthday, John!"

"Sorry to be so late, Howard."

"Car trouble?"

"Yes—nothing serious. My husband took care of it."

I always mean well but I guess I try to do too much in too little time—with too little concentration.

Dear Lord, I know I didn't tell Howard the exact truth about it, but it was car trouble. I'm trying to be a good witness, and wouldn't they think anything I say about You is dopey if I can't remember not to lock the keys in the trunk?

"Be very careful, then, how you live—not as unwise

129

but as wise, making the most of every opportunity, because the days are evil. Therefore do not be foolish, but understand what the Lord's will is" (Ephesians 5:15-17).

Higher-Oops

"Hello, Mother?"

"Yes honey, is something wrong?"

"No, I have something exciting to tell you and couldn't wait until tonight to call."

"Oh good!"

"Remember when I told you that Gene Wright, the division head, went to Saudi Arabia?"

"The one you gave a tract?"

"That's the one—"

"I've been praying for him."

"Good, Mother. Anyway, the reason I called—Mr. Ellsworth, he's the man who is filling in for Mr. Wright until they hire a new man, needs a secretary. See, the girl who was Mr. Wright's secretary took a better job. So all of us, the secretaries in Personnel, have been taking turns doing Mr. Ellsworth's work."

"Uhummm."

"Christy, the girl who sits next to me, wants me to apply for the job, but I told her no—"

"Why not?" Mother asked.

"Because. It's too disappointing when you don't get it."

"Shame on you, honey."

"Well! I'm not trying for a big career. But listen! Mr. Ellsworth called me into his office just a few minutes ago and told me he liked the way I work and wants me to be his secretary!"

"Oh, how wonderful! Is it definite?"

"Sure. He said it was just a formality to put it through Job Posting, then the Vice President has to sign it. Oh, Mother! Isn't it exciting? And I didn't even have to apply for the job!"

"Sit down, Mab. Well, it's been two weeks since we talked."

"Yes! I'm still walking on air, Mr. Ellsworth."

"Y-e-e-s. Well. We have a problem. It seems the higher-ups don't want you to be my secretary. Now wait a minute—no reflection on your ability. As expected, they have finally hired a man to take this desk and I'll be going back to my old desk. The general opinion upstairs is that the new man should be allowed to hire his own secretary. In fact, he may bring his present secretary with him.

"So . . . I guess Howard gets to keep you after all."

Pain! G-r-r-h! (Don't cry, stupid!) I *hate* them all!

Lord! What are You doing to me? What are You trying to teach me?

"In his heart a man plans his course, but the Lord determines his steps" (Proverbs 16:9).

Brighten the Corner

"Would you believe I had all this stuff in my purse?" I pointed to a big mound of assorted junk in the center of the kitchen table. My neighbor shook her head, apparently speechless.

"No wonder my shoulders ache."

She sat down across from me. "Could I ask you a question?"

I nodded as I separated stuff to keep from stuff to throw away.

"Do you actually use all that equipment?" She snickered.

I picked up a small hairbrush. "The last time I got my hair cut the beautician sold me this, but I have to confess I always use my comb."

"How about that can of hairspray?"

"Never use it anymore."

"That tube of medicine?"

"I used to put that on a spot of eczema—but it's gone now, thank the Lord."

"What's the roll of nickels for?"

"I mean to turn those in to the bank but I keep forgetting."

"Oh, you've got pictures; may I see them?"

"You have. They're the ones I took Easter."

"Easter!" She laughed. "It's only October. And what are those pieces of paper?"

"They're words to songs. Christian songs. There's a sweet girl at work—May, is her name—she runs the automatic typewriter. Ever since she found out I am a Christian she always scribbles out the words to a song and attaches it to my work. She must know a million songs. She always signs herself, 'Song Bandit.' You can't imagine what a lift it gives me."

I picked up one of the papers. "Take this one, for instance. She put this on my work the day Mr. Ellsworth told me I wasn't going to get the job with him. I think it's called 'Heartaches.' Listen:

'Heartaches, take them all to Jesus,
Go to Him today, do it now without delay;
Heartaches, take them all to Jesus,
He will take your heartaches all away.'

"Isn't that amazing? She didn't know anything about my heartache at the time."

"That really is amazing," my neighbor said.

"She is really a corner brightener. Another thing, her husband isn't interested in spiritual matters, but even though she has only been married about a year she goes to church every Sunday by herself."

My neighbor sipped her coffee.

"That would take real courage," she finally said. "Or faith." She stared out the kitchen window for quite awhile and I wondered what she was thinking. She picked up the scrap of paper and read the words again.

"You know what?" she asked, and her chin lifted. "I think I'll go to church with you next Sunday— even if my husband doesn't want to go."

May! You think you're too shy to be a witness but look what you've done!

Dear Lord, thank You for my neighbor's decision. Please keep her strong in courage and faith to do what she said. And thank You for little May's song, for all her songs.

"Sing joyfully to the Lord . . . it is fitting . . . to praise him. Praise the Lord . . . make music to him . . . Sing to him a new song . . ." (Psalm 33:1,2,3).

"Speak to one another with psalms, hymns and spiritual songs . . ." (Ephesians 5:19).

Trick or Treat

"Isn't it enough that you're always making cookies for the people at work without making hundreds of cookies for handouts?" my husband grumbled the night before Halloween.

"It won't take too long," I said as I dropped dough on the cookie sheets. "I'll even give you one. Besides, you can help."

"I was afraid of that."

"See those little orange and black sacks over there? How about opening them and putting them on the table. Please? Then put a Halloween tract in each one." He stood up slowly.

"Do you really think any of the kids read them? Last year there were at least a dozen of them on the lawn. They took the candy and threw the tracts down."

"I know. That's the reason for the sacks. We can put the cookies and tracts inside and staple the top of the sack. Maybe they'll wait until they get home to open them. I'm going to take some of them to work too."

"Handouts or tracts?"

"Both." He shook his head.

"Bonnie says on Halloween they all bring handouts and wear orange and black."

"My word. Do you work for a business organization or a social club?"

"I'll let you take some to your office."

"I'm not going to start that. It's hard enough to support your crew."

"I'm going to put the tracts beside the cookies on my desk. If anyone wants to pick one up, he can."

"So . . . was it trick or treat?" my husband asked at dinner that night.

"Every cookie was devoured by nine o'clock, but I only had one taker on the tracts."

"Who was it?"

"Bertha—my black friend. I really like her. She's very intelligent; in fact she's studying to get her C.P.A. and she has her own business, some kind of management consulting firm or something. But it isn't quite enough to support her two boys yet. We have talked quite a bit about faith and she definitely believes in God and prayer, but I'm not sure if she believes she is a sinner and needs Christ. I hope she'll understand the tract better than my garbled testimony."

"Well, God can make her understand. We'll pray for her."

"I want to do more. When we do our income tax next year can we let her do it?"

My husband looked aghast.

135

"Are you sure she can?"

"Positive. Besides, what better way to demonstrate Christ's love than to help her? She's a widow."

"Okay." He sighed. "I guess if Paul witnessed in jail I can too."

What is that little motto? "Only one life 'twill soon be past—only what's done for Christ will last."

Dear Lord, the more I know these dear people in Personnel the more I want them all to be saved. Please work on Bertha.

"I have become all things to all men so that by all possible means I might save some" (I Corinthians 9:22b).

Promotion

"Pss-s-t!"

I looked over at Christy. She motioned for me to scoot over to her. She pointed at a Job Posting notice she had just typed. It was for a Senior Secretary.

"Christy, I told you I'm not going to apply anymore!"

"But this is for secretary to Karen Harper, right here in Overseas Personnel. It's a great opportunity. You'd be the same as Marlene."

136

"Forget it, okay? I appreciate your encouragement, Christy, but . . . no!"

She shrugged.

"You white folks sho am dumb."

Later in the day I went to the restroom—and there was Karen Harper. As long as I had worked at Jenkins, Karen and I had never been in the restroom at the same time. No one else was in the room, so I sat down in an easy chair next to her. It was natural to talk to her.

"I understand Juanita is leaving," I said.

"Not leaving," Karen answered. "She's being promoted in the department." Karen took a sip of Coke, then a puff of her cigarette. She was about twenty-eight, tall and big-boned, but slender. She wore her black hair in a short page-boy, and aside from a touch of eyeshadow over electric-blue eyes, she wore no make-up. She looked athletic, but she could have been a model.

"So now you'll be needing a secretary?"

She nodded one short nod.

"Would you consider me?"

There was a flicker of amusement in her eyes.

"Certainly. Tell me about yourself."

I told her about working in the bookstore, and when I was secretary to an attorney, and the time I was pastor's secretary. I also told her about my two disappointments at Jenkins.

"Maybe I'm a poor sport but I don't want to apply for another job. I would enjoy a change, though, so if you don't find anyone you like better, I'm available!" I smiled at her and she gave me a Mona Lisa smile.

I didn't tell anyone I had talked to Karen, not even my husband. Two days later Karen telephoned.

137

"Come back to my office."

I felt as though someone was holding a thumb on my throat. Trembling slightly I sat down opposite her.

"Still want the job?"

"Yes."

"I've cleared it with Job Posting. It's yours."

I was shaking hard. I glanced out her office door to the door of *my* office. How marvelous! How scary.

When the Lord decides to move, *He moves.*

Dear Lord, I know there is a reason for me to work for Karen. Help me, help me to be a good secretary. Please don't let me do dumb things. Thank You for this promotion.

"No one from the east or the west or from the desert can exalt a man. But it is God who judges; he brings one down, he exalts another" (Psalm 75:6,7).

Happiness Is Finding Charlie Brown

Yesterday was Thanksgiving Day and we had a wonderful time. All the food was extra good and it was great to be with the entire family. At the table we took turns telling what we were most thankful for. I didn't mention it yesterday, but aside from salvation and my husband, I think I am most thankful to have an extra day off.

I got the kitchen cleaned up early this morning and then took off for the mall to start Christmas shopping. So far I've made about as much progress as a person going up a down escalator.

The problem is that all the people in my family have such definite ideas about what they want; brands, colors, styles. What I can't figure out is where they get their information. Almost everything on my Christmas list is something no clerk has ever heard of.

For instance, one of the teenagers wants "twisted gold loop earrings, about the size of a nickel." I found them the size of a penny, dime, quarter and fifty cents. One little guy on my list wants a Charlie Brown watch. I found Snoopy, Lucy and Peanuts. Charlie—where are you?

My sister wants a certain size and brand stainless steel cooking pan. I finally found the exact item in the housewares section of an exclusive department store. In spite of the crowds everywhere else, I was the only customer in this department. Two ultra-refined sales persons strolled silently on the thick carpet, eyeing me with suspicion. I felt self-conscious, tacky, and more awkward than usual.

The utensils were displayed like treasures on glass shelves, interspersed with expensive Christmas ornaments.

I looked at the pan I wanted to buy, then carefully reached out to lift the lid. It stuck to the pan and the entire unit lifted about an inch, then dropped with an ear-shattering clang.

As I grabbed for it the lid bonged against the shelf above and sent ornaments spinning to the carpet. One clerk rushed toward me with her eyes and mouth open.

"Oh my goodness! May I help you? *Please?*"

I bought the pan. That's one gift I can scratch off the list. As for the earrings, watch, lavender Dittos, and pink roller skates, at least I know where they aren't.

No matter how hectic—and it will be hectic this year with me working—I still love Christmas.

Dear Lord, with inflation and so little time to shop help me buy every Christmas gift. May whatever I buy somehow be to Thy glory.

"He [Joseph] went there to register with Mary, who was pledged to be married to him and was expecting a child. While they were there, the time came for the baby to be born, and she gave birth to her firstborn, a son. She wrapped him in strips of cloth and placed him in a manger, because there was no room for them in the inn" (Luke 2:5-7).

First the Bad News

"How was your day?" my husband asked. "You seem kind of down." He sat down in his chair, and I sat on the couch.

"Oh—I got some good news, and some bad news."

"Better tell me the bad news first."

"It was pretty humiliating. I sort of got bawled out today."

He put down the evening paper and looked at me. Then he got up and came to sit by me.

"Poor baby. Tell me about it."

"Every Friday night Karen calls a department staff meeting, and since I'm her secretary it's my job to notify everyone. It's time consuming to go to every person and say, 'Staff meeting at four,' especially when everyone always groans, 'Oh no!'

"So I thought I was pretty efficient when I thought of putting a notice up on the bulletin board. Instead of typing a dry old notice I drew a picture of this idiotic-looking character with his eyes crossed and his tongue hanging out, with the words, 'Staff Meeting, 4:00 o'clock.' "

My husband whistled. "Not too dignified."

"I know it!" I flared. "But nobody sees the bulletin board except our department.'"

"So what happened?"

"Juanita—she's the one who used to be Karen's secretary—called me into her office and showed me the cartoon.

" 'Babe,' she said, 'I know you didn't mean any harm,' and she looked at me like I was a two-year-old, 'but Karen didn't like this. Said it wasn't profes-

141

sional and it was a reflection on her office. Don't do it again.' "

My husband put his arm around me and held me close while I tried to keep from crying.

"I think the reason I feel so badly is because one morning last week Juanita was really down; she's getting a divorce and I gave her a rose and a salvation tract, and told her I was praying for her. Now with this one dumb thing I've blown my testimony."

"I think you're making too much out of it. The Lord will handle it. You'll see." He reached over to the candy dish and took out an orange slice. "What was the good news?"

I brightened as I thought of it.

"They want me to write a Christmas play, a skit! Personnel always has a luncheon and party—*no* drinks—and they want to have a program this year. I only have two weeks to get it written, then they'll have about a week to get the program together. Isn't that exciting? I told them I'd do it if they would let me put in a line or two about the true meaning of Christmas."

"Good for you! What did they say?"

"Oh sure. Everybody knows that Christ was born. I hope I can make the skit funny yet potent."

Me, professional? I'm afraid I just ain't got no "salve-war fare."

Lord, help me to live moment by moment with You. If I had asked You first, You would have warned me not to draw the cartoon. Help me now Lord, with the words for the skit—funny lines, yet a way to tell about Your birth.

"Each one should use whatever gift he has received to serve others, faithfully administering God's grace in its various forms...he should do it with the strength God provides, so that in all things God may be praised through Jesus Christ" (I Peter 4:10,11a).

Nuttiest Fruit Cake of All

"Since you're working I don't guess you'll be doing any baking this Christmas will you?" my mother asked yesterday.

"I don't know."

"I was hoping you would make the same fruit cake you made last year." She rubbed her stomach and smacked her lips. "That was the best I've ever eaten."

"Really?"

"If you have the recipe maybe I could bake it."

The recipe? I closed my eyes and sighed as I remembered.

The recipe for "Blue Ribbon Fruit Cake" called for white syrup and I didn't have any, so I had used Bre'r Rabbit Molasses. I had the candied citron, pineapple and cherries it called for, but no orange, so

I had put in a handful of candy orange slices. I didn't have a pint of peach brandy either, so I had used a jar of peach jam. I had the dates required but no raisins, so I had used a package of prunes, which unfortunately I had already stewed. But all in all, it seemed to me these were reasonable substitutions, and it had beat going to the store.

The cakes—two loaf pans, three coffee cans and a jello mold—had to be baked in a pan of water at 250 degrees for about two-and-a-half hours, or until done.

After the time limit the house smelled like a bakery and I was starved, but when I took the cakes out to cool I resisted even a taste until dinner that night.

"This pudding's not too shabby," my husband said, forking in a big mouthful of soft stuff.

"It's not pudding," I had cried and snatched it away from him.

There was no alternative but to grease all the pans again and put the 'puddings' back in the oven. I let them cook all through Lawrence Welk, then we began to smell burned sugar. When I saw those dark, dark brown things in the oven I was ready to throw them out, but when I counted the cost in time and money I decided to let them cool until morning.

Next morning, using our sharpest butcher knife and barber scissors, I cut away the burned parts, put each dry cake in a plastic bag and poured grape juice on them. I sealed the bags and stuck them in the refrigerator.

I had brought them out for our family get-together on Christmas Eve, and to my amazement almost every soggy crumb was wolfed down.

My little mother doesn't ask many favors of me, so I decided to try it again. I'm beginning to smell the

144

burned sugar now.

When will I ever learn to follow a recipe exactly?

Dear Lord, You have shown me something else. Not only am I unwilling to follow recipes but there are times when I think the rules were made for the other fellow.

"Hold on to instruction, do not let it go; guard it well, for it is your life . . . pay attention to what I say; listen closely to my words" (Proverbs 4:13,20).

A Tale of Two Lunches

There have been two special lunch hours for me this week. The first was with Bea Simpson. I can't get over how different she seems since the first Bible class we attended. Her green eyes sparkle and she's losing weight. She seems so alive and beautiful.

"You're losing weight," I remarked at lunch. "How are you doing it?"

Her eyes crinkled and her mouth curved in a pleased smile.

"I've wanted to tell you for quite awhile but I wanted to be sure. The way I've lost so much weight is, *I've quit drinking!*"

I drew in my breath with excitement.

"Or rather," she added quickly, "the Lord has taken away the desire."

"Praise the Lord!"

"I didn't admit it to you, and hardly to myself, but I've had a serious drinking problem. I could hardly wait to get home at night to have anywhere from two cocktails to—who knows? Now it's coffee, tea or milk!" She laughed happily. Then her smile died.

"The next thing is these." She held up the ever-present burning cigarette. "That's why I wanted to have lunch with you. You've helped me so much by your prayers. Now I want you to pray especially hard. January one is the cut-off date."

The other special lunch was with Ann Valdemar from Cost Planning.

"Congratulations!" she said on the phone early one morning. At first I couldn't place the voice.

"Congratulations for what?" I said.

"Your new position, silly." Then I knew it was Ann. "Isn't it about time we have that lunch date? How about today? I'll meet you by the escalator ten minutes early."

Fortunately I had nothing planned that couldn't be changed. We briskly walked three blocks to her favorite restaurant. After we were seated I tried to relax. I wished I felt more at ease and less like a clod-hopper. I also kept stuttering, but I doubt if she noticed because she did most of the talking.

"So, I have reservations for Mazatlan. Then in March I plan to go to Hawaii—sort of a drag because I've been there so many times but my sis wants me to go. I want to go to Tahiti, and positively I shall go

146

next year. What are you going to do on your vacation?"

"I'm not sure—probably stay home."

She raised her brows and slipped a beautifully manicured finger under the gold necklace she always wore. She also wore expensive rings on *every* finger.

"I wouldn't be caught dead in costume jewelry," she had said once to Alice.

While she talked about how incompetent most of Personnel was, I wondered what I was doing here. We had nothing in common. She was divorced, liberated, self-made and apparently extremely content. I was sure there was nothing in my life that was of interest to her.

Suddenly she asked, "What church do you belong to?"

I jerked to attention. *(Lord, help me not to blow it.)*

"We go to a neat church, but I hesitate to name it. Brands aren't important."

"What do you mean?"

"It's the Person who is important—Jesus Christ. Any church who puts Him at the top is okay."

"Well, I never heard that before. My church kicked me out when I got divorced, and I figured, brother, if they don't need me, I don't need them."

"Well," I said timidly, "in a way you *don't* need them." *(Oh you chicken, everybody needs the fellowship of the Body.)* "But you *do* need Christ—God, you know." I looked up at her ice-blue eyes, then looked at my salad.

"Ann, Jim Jorgensen teaches a great Bible class. Would you come sometime?"

She let out a war-whoop laugh you could hear all over the restaurant.

"Oh, my friend!" she said. "I would really know I was bored if I ever agreed to go to a Bible class!"

Two women, almost the same age. One has received, the other is still deceived.

Dear Lord, please release Your power in Bea to overcome the cigarettes. And Lord, please soften Ann. Let her forget the bad times in the first church and see Jesus only.

"Then a cloud appeared and enveloped them, and a voice came from the cloud: 'This is my Son, whom I love. Listen to him!' Suddenly, when they looked around, they no longer saw anyone with them except Jesus" (Mark 9:7,8).

A Special Place

"Don't forget the Christmas decorations Monday," Bonnie told everyone. When she stopped at my office she said, "This is your first Christmas at Jenkins, isn't it?"

"Yes! I'm looking forward to it."

"We always bring decorations from home and decorate our desks. It's really beautiful around here. Then on the day of the lunch and program, we take the stuff into the conference room and decorate."

That night I took down all our Christmas decorations to see what I could spare to take to work.

There were the green and red ceramic elves the kids had given me when they were little, and the new crystal ornament a girlfriend had given me last year. The tree-top star looked more elegant than I remembered, and the ornament I had put on every tree since I was a girl was still unbroken.

But what could I take to work? I kept looking, poking through old tissue paper, and finally underneath an extension cord and some old icicles I found the little plastic figures we had used when we were first married. A couple of years ago they had been replaced by a more elegant set, but this year, I decided, there would be a special place on my desk for *the nativity*.

I wonder if the set will offend the Moslems, Jews or atheists at Jenkins?

Lord Jesus, it is the day we celebrate Your birthday. Let these little figures make everyone pause for a moment and think of Your birth.

" '... Do not be afraid. I bring you good news of great joy that will be for all the people. Today in the town of David a Savior has been born to you; he is Christ the Lord' " (Luke 2:10b,11).

The Play's the Thing

"Mother, you want to see some Polaroid pictures of the skit I wrote being performed?"

"That's right; that was yesterday, wasn't it? How did it go?"

"Real well. I wouldn't say this to anyone else but it was so thrilling to hear the 'actors' say the lines I wrote!"

"I remember the feeling. I wrote a play for P.T.A. once."

"You did? I didn't know that. I guess that's where I get this urge to write. What was thrilling to me was that the lines I thought were funny made the audience roar! It was a delicious sound!"

"Careful, there. That's the old ego!"

"Do you think it's ego when you pray to be used of the Lord and ask Him to give you the ability? Honestly, Mother, I give Him all the praise but at the same time I couldn't help but be happy when everyone seemed to like it."

I handed her the pictures. "That first one is really the last. That's where they presented me with an autographed copy of the script."

"These are good pictures. Did you put in anything about the Lord?"

"Not much, but a little. See this picture where Jim is looking down at the receptionist? And see the little Christmas tree? Well, Jim says, 'Mitzi, I see you have your tree decorated. Do you know why we decorate at Christmas?' Then he goes on to tell about Christ's birth, the Prince of Peace. He gives us the gift of peace—which means peace of mind today; and

150

that's why we give gifts and decorate. It's a celebration, His birthday.

"Then one of the secretaries comes in and says, 'Birthday? Don't tell me I forgot to bring goodies.' Everybody laughed then."

"Sounds like a pretty good skit, honey."

"I'm glad it's over, in a way. I was almost a nervous wreck!"

What scrumptious agony. I felt like a mother at a piano recital.

Lord Jesus, forgive me if this feeling is egotistical. I know You could stamp out my life as easily as I step on a bug. I give You the honor and You can have the autographed script, if You want it.

" . . . I hate pride and arrogance . . ." (Proverbs 8:13).

"Therefore God exalted him to the highest place and gave him the name that is above every name, that at the name of Jesus every knee should bow, in heaven and on earth . . . and every tongue confess that Jesus Christ is Lord, to the glory of God the Father" (Philippians 2:9-11).

New Year's Revolutions

"Happy New Year, darling," I said.

"Happy New Year to you. Well, what are your resolutions?"

"Are you kidding?" I scoffed. "I gave that up years ago."

"You mean you're not even going to try to be a better person?"

"Are you?"

"Sure. I'm going to quit eating liver. That in itself will help my disposition."

"Oh, those kinds. Okay, I'll think of some resolutions." In awhile I handed him a sheet of paper.

1. Housekeeping shows up many flaws in my character. For example, every week I feel compelled to vacuum, dust, change sheets, wash clothes. I now see this as basic *wilfulness*. So in the coming year I'm going to clean house less often, thereby demonstrating a more relaxed me.

2. Every weekend I spend a lot of time on my wardrobe trying to decide what to wear with what the following week. That's practicing *divination*. We aren't supposed to predict the future so no more trying to guess what I'll be wearing.

3. My hair has been another show of character weakness. I continue to blow-dry it just so I can be in style, even though flat hair makes me look like Kojak. That's pure *faddism*. I'm going to give away my blow-dryer and find my curlers.

4. I like for the LTD to be clean so that it won't be the only one in the lot that looks as though it's camouflaged for war maneuvers. That's nothing but

pride. That trait must go so I'm through washing the car.

5. Putting out guest towels has shown me another despicable facet in my character. I put those towels out just to prove I have them. Pure *exhibitionism*. I'll never put out another guest towel. Nobody uses them anyhow.

6. The basic reason I don't want to get fat is because I want other people to think I look nice. That's *vanity*. So, for the sake of improving my character I'm giving up all diets in the new year.

After he had read the list my husband nodded his approval.

"I'm glad to see you're still willing to try to be a better person."

I do want to be a better person but every time my wings start to grow, my horns get in the way.

Dear Lord, because I have made so many resolutions and then broken them, I'm not going to make any. But I ask You to be the Lord of my life every day of this new year.

"It is better not to vow than to make a vow and not fulfill it" (Ecclesiastes 5:5).

The Writer?

I talked to the boss on the Wat's line this morning," my husband announced one evening at dinner.

"What did he have to say?" I poured coffee. I wasn't sure I wanted to hear what his boss had to say. I had felt for a long time that my husband carried too much responsibility for too little pay, at least according to Jenkins' pay schedules.

"Well, for one thing, they're going to close the office up north and work out of our plant exclusively."

"What will that mean? You'll be working harder?"

"Probably. But—" his eyes gleamed. "I've been promoted. That means a substantial raise." He took a sip of coffee and went on. "So, you asked what it means, the most important thing to me is you can quit work."

I sat down quietly and began to have an imaginary conversation with my new boss, Karen. "I don't know how to tell you this—" Good grief. I was just getting settled in my new job. What would she think?

"It will have to be your decision," my husband said. "But I want you to know if *you* want to stay home I want you to."

So many times I had thought how glad I would be when the bills were caught up and I could once again be a homemaker—and writer. Now the time had come if I wanted it. But there was a lot to consider. I made a good salary and I had a certain amount of prestige as Karen's secretary. Working conditions were good. I felt confident and assured—and how unconfident and unassured I felt with each publisher's rejection slip! What made me think I could write anyhow?

"Personally, I think you can write," my husband said as though reading my mind. "You've sold enough to show that. I think you can write a best-seller!"

Tears came to my eyes. More than anything writing was what I wanted to do.

"Pray for me, okay?" I said.

While the meatloaf got cold he prayed that I would only do what the Lord wanted me to do.

After dinner I stood up and looked at the calendar. The peace that honestly passes understanding filled me.

"If I quit at the end of this month," I said, "it will give Karen three weeks to find another secretary. I'm going to tell her tomorrow."

Homemaker vs. Businesswoman. Senior Secretary vs. Writer. Have I made the right choice?

Dear Lord, I know You found my job for me at Jenkins, and I praise You. Now I thank You that it's over and I can begin another phase of service.

"... teach the ... women to ... love their husbands and children, to be self-controlled and pure, to be busy at home, to be kind, and to be subject to their husbands ..." (Titus 2:3-5).

Last Day

On my last day Karen called me into her office.

"I want to take you to lunch today," she said. "We took you at your word. You said you didn't want a farewell party and it's a good thing. Everyone is so busy on the new contract."

I nodded. It was a madhouse, trying to get people processed as fast as they were needed.

"But at least I wanted us to have lunch together," she said. I felt a tiny stab of disappointment. I *had* said I didn't want a big to-do made over me. I hadn't been her secretary long enough for that. Yet I had secretly hoped they would plan *something* for me.

Then another thought came to me. I had never had the opportunity to tell Karen about Jesus Christ. Maybe that's why we were supposed to have lunch together.

It was raining when we hurried to her little sports car. It was intimate and cozy inside and it seemed all right to ask her some personal questions.

"Karen, how did you become an Overseas Personnel boss?"

"It is amazing, isn't it?" she said with her usual dry wit. "Well, let's see. First of all, in college I majored in French. I was going to teach French. I had spent about a year in France when I suddenly became disenchanted with the whole scene."

"Why? It seems such a romantic place."

"It wasn't the country. It was me. I just didn't want to be a teacher."

"What a shame—all that language background."

"I know. That's my only regret. I speak it fluently. Now there's no need."

"You could be a missionary," I said. I looked at her out of the corner of my eye.

She was silent and all I could hear was the frantic swish-swish of the windshield wipers.

"I was brought up in the Lutheran church," she said about a block later.

My heart leaped. "Then you know all about Jesus Christ dying for your—our sins?"

"Yes."

The conversation stopped. Well, I didn't need to pursue it. She said she knew all about it, didn't she?"

"Karen, I didn't want to bring religion into our relationship but this is my last day, and I can't leave without telling you what Jesus Christ has done for me."

I gave her a *Reader's Digest* version of my testimony. She was polite but seemed unmoved.

"Karen, you have everything going for you now, but if you're ever in a jam call on Jesus. He's ready and waiting and able to solve your problems."

I had just finished when we pulled into a—a pizza palace?

When we walked in the door a great, resounding roar went up:

"*Surprise!*"

The whole place was filled with Jenkins personnel. Everywhere I looked was someone I knew. I couldn't believe it. They pulled me to a table in the center of the room and I sat with Mr. Ellsworth, Howard and Karen. There was a huge cake on the table with a message: "Good Luck, Mab." I unwrapped a beautiful big suit box, only to find another box, and another, and another until at last I reached a tiny jeweler's box which contained a fifteen inch gold

157

chain. Tears blinded me. I had to get Bonnie to fasten it.

I was Cinderella at the ball. I was a princess. It was too fantastic to be real.

All afternoon people stopped by with gifts; everything from homemade cookies to a pair of 14K gold cross earrings. Why? Why? I still don't know why. I only know it was overwhelming.

I am not worthy of so much attention and so many gifts.

Lord Jesus, not only am I not worthy of all this earthly attention but I realize again that I am not worthy of all You have done for me. You died for me so that I could live for You, but most of the time I've lived for myself.

"But thanks be to God, who always leads us in triumphal procession in Christ and through us spreads everywhere the fragrance of the knowledge of him. For we are to God the aroma of Christ among those who are being saved and those who are perishing. To the one we are the smell of death; to the other, the fragrance of life. And who is equal to such a task?" (II Corinthians 2:14-16).

Bulletin

"Hi Mab? How you like staying home?"

"Who is this? Christy?"

"It's me. I wanted to tell you I'm thinking about getting married."

"Are you in love?"

"Mmmmmm-hmm!"

"You may think I'm dopey—"

"Right!"

"But don't leave God out of your marriage this time. He loves you and wants to do everything wonderful for you."

"I know."

"Why don't you and your fiance come see us?"

"We will! Say—did you hear about Juanita?"

"Karen's secretary before you pushed me into that job?"

"Yeah. She was killed in an automobile accident. Killed instantly."

Juanita! I thought of the rose and the salvation tract. Thank You, Lord.

Epilogue

The telephone rang right in the middle of a chapter. I was tempted to let it ring, but . . .

"Hello?"

"Mab? This is Cindy."

"Cindy? Oh! Cindy at Jenkins! Hi! How you doing?"

"I'm fine! Guess what?"

"You're engaged?"

"You're getting close!"

"You're not married?"

"Mab! I thought you'd guess right away."

"I can't guess. Tell me."

"I accepted Christ Saturday night."

I was so happy, so shocked, so amazed I could only babble "Oh, oh, oh."

"It was at a youth rally. And I'm going to be baptized. I want you and your husband to come if you can. I just had to tell you because of all the little religious messages you used to give me! I knew you'd be glad."